English for Business Studies

A course for Business Studies and Economics students

Third Edition

Teacher's Book

Ian MacKenzie

CAMBRIDGE
UNIVERSITY PRESS

University Printing House, Cambridge CB2 8BS, United Kingdom

Cambridge University Press is part of the University of Cambridge.

It furthers the University's mission by disseminating knowledge in the pursuit of education, learning and research at the highest international levels of excellence.

www.cambridge.org
Information on this title: www.cambridge.org/9780521743426

© Cambridge University Press 2010

This publication is in copyright. Subject to statutory exception and to the provisions of relevant collective licensing agreements, no reproduction of any part may take place without the written permission of Cambridge University Press.

First published 1997
Second edition 2002
Third edition 2010
5th printing 2014

A catalogue record for this publication is available from the British Library

ISBN 978-0-521-74341-9 Student's Book
ISBN 978-0-521-74342-6 Teacher's Book
ISBN 978-0-521-74343-3 Audio CD Set

Cambridge University Press has no responsibility for the persistence or accuracy of URLs for external or third-party internet websites referred to in this publication, and does not guarantee that any content on such websites is, or will remain, accurate or appropriate.

Contents

Introduction	4
Map of the book	7
List of role cards in the Student's Book	10

Management

1 Management	12
2 Work and motivation	15
3 Company structure	20
4 Managing across cultures	23
5 Recruitment	28
6 Women in business	34

Production

7 The different sectors of the economy	37
8 Production	41
9 Logistics	44
10 Quality	48

Marketing

11 Products	52
12 Marketing	56
13 Advertising	60

Finance

14 Banking	65
15 Venture capital	69
16 Bonds	72
17 Stocks and shares	76
18 Derivatives	80
19 Accounting and financial statements	84
20 Market structure and competition	88
21 Takeovers	93

Economics

22 Government and taxation	97
23 The business cycle	101
24 Corporate social responsibility	105
25 Efficiency and employment	109
26 Exchange rates	112
27 International trade	115
28 Economics and ecology	119
Thanks and acknowledgements	125

Introduction

English for Business Studies is an upper-intermediate to advanced level reading, listening, speaking and writing course (Common European Framework for Languages levels B2–C2) for learners who need to understand and express the key concepts of business and economics in English. It covers the most important areas of management, production, marketing, finance and macroeconomics.

It consists of a Student's Book, two Audio CDs and this Teacher's Book. The Student's Book contains 28 units, role cards, audio scripts of the listening material, and appendices on presenting and writing. This Teacher's Book contains guidance on using the material, commentaries on the business concepts presented, answers to the exercises, and the audio scripts.

The aims of *English for Business Studies* are:
- to present your students with the language and concepts of business and economics found in books, journals, newspapers and magazines, and on websites
- to build vocabulary through reading, listening and speaking
- to develop reading skills and give practice in the comprehension of business and economics texts
- to develop listening skills, using interviews with business people, economists and other experts
- to improve speaking skills, confidence and fluency, and to provide learners with opportunities to express business concepts themselves, while synthesizing, summarizing, analysing, criticizing and discussing ideas
- to develop writing skills.

Unit structure

Most of the units contain four components:
1. An informative reading text giving an overview of a particular topic, introducing key concepts and including a high density of relevant technical vocabulary, plus a variety of comprehension and vocabulary exercises and discussion activities. These texts are designed to spare teachers (and learners) the task of finding for themselves the wide range of articles or texts from other sources that would be necessary to cover all the requisite ground. There are also extracts from newspapers, books about business and economics, and a novel, which use more idiomatic language.
2. Listening passages, and comprehension, vocabulary and discussion exercises, largely based on interviews with business people and economists. The interviewees include MBA students at the University of Cambridge, professors of business, economics and science, a banker, a computing consultant, a hotel manager, the manager of a chain of juice bars, an IT director, a journalist and writer, a venture capitalist, and regulators from the Competition Commission and the Financial Services Authority in the UK. There are also authentic US radio commercials and (scripted) radio business news reports. The listening material includes British, American, Australian and South African voices, but also speakers from several European and Asian countries. It is important that learners get used to hearing a variety of native and non-native speakers of English, as this is what international business people encounter in their professional lives.

3 Speaking activities including discussions, case studies, role plays and presentations. These are designed to give the learners the opportunity to discuss the ideas in the reading and listening material and to play a role or develop and defend their own points of view.

4 Writing activities including summaries, emails, memos and reports.

There are two Appendices at the back of the Student's Book:
- how to give a good presentation
- writing emails, letters and reports.

Approach to the units

The units are grouped thematically in five sections: management, production, marketing, finance and economics. The different groups of units are not graded in terms of difficulty, and so need not necessarily be followed in the printed order, but vocabulary items and concepts included in earlier units are not glossed when recycled in later ones.

The units begin with lead-in questions for discussion. The reading passages are also generally preceded by discussion questions. These preliminary discussion activities can easily be extended, with the teacher eliciting information from the learners, if they are familiar with the topic, and guiding the discussion according to the content of the text, thereby preparing for and greatly simplifying the subsequent reading task. The trick of teaching specialized areas of a language is to use the learners as a resource whenever possible. If there are time constraints, some of the reading passages could also be assigned as homework.

Nearly all the discussion activities are designed to be done by pairs or small groups of learners, according to the teacher's preferences. Although it is not printed on every page, the instruction 'Discuss in pairs or small groups' is implicit. Some of the speaking activities (presentations, role plays and case studies) involve out-of-class preparation and group work.

Each unit is designed to provide two or three hours of work. The book offers enough material for a two-hours-a-week course lasting a single academic year.

The Third Edition

This new edition covers much of the same ground as the previous editions, but has been updated as the world of business and economics does not stand still. Most of the texts in the earlier editions have been revised or replaced. All the listening material is new, as are many of the speaking activities (not to mention the cartoons and artwork). Some of the material that was previously spread over two units has now been combined in a single unit. Conversely, where there was previously one unit on production there are now four. The former Unit 1 now opens the production section.

The unit on IT in the Second Edition has gone as computers are now *everywhere*, from wikinomics (in Unit 3) to automated supply chains and sorting offices (Units 8, 9 and 25) to viral marketing (Unit 13) to online trading (Unit 17). In fact the main difference between writing this edition and the first one 15 years ago is that this time I didn't need to cut out promising articles and put them in a file and go to libraries to find books that often contained out-of-date information, but merely spent a lot of time online. This book (and many others now being written) should really be dedicated to all the people who made the Internet, the worldwide web, archives and search engines possible.

Although coursebooks such as this are designed to save teachers the trouble of finding articles and texts about business subjects, it is now possible to find and download material complementing any subject covered in this book. Given the speed at which things change, this may occasionally be advisable.

I hope you enjoy using this book with your learners. Feedback is welcome, via http://www.cambridge.org/elt.

Professional English Online

You may find it useful to visit Professional English Online, a website for teachers and trainers of business English and English for Special Purposes. You'll find more on *English for Business Studies* at the site, along with a range of other free activities, podcasts, blogs and competitions on a range of business English topics.

Visit http://peo.cambridge.org.

Map of the book

Unit		Reading	Listening	Speaking	Writing
1	Management	What is management?	MBA students: What makes a good manager?	Case study: Selecting a Chief Operating Officer	Summary; email
2	Work and motivation	Theory X and Theory Y; 'Satisfiers' and 'motivators'	MBA students: Managers and motivation	Case study: A car manufacturer	Summary; email
3	Company structure	Wikinomics and the future of companies; Company structure	MBA students: Big and small companies	Presentation: Presenting a company	Notes for a presentation
4	Managing across cultures	Managing across cultures	MBA students: Managers, authority, and cultural diversity	Role play: Welcoming American colleagues	Autobiographical text
5	Recruitment	Filling a vacancy; Job applications	John Antonakis (management professor): Job interviews	Role play: A job interview	Curriculum vitae or resume
6	Women in business	You're fired! (The Guardian)	Alison Maitland (writer and journalist): Women in business – a strategic issue	Role play: Do we need more women managers?	Memo or email
7	The different sectors of the economy	Another cup of tea (David Lodge: Nice Work); Manufacturing and services	The business news (radio)	Discussion: Your place in the economy	Business news item
8	Production	Capacity and inventory; 'The Dell Theory of Conflict Prevention' (Thomas Friedman: The World Is Flat)	Alan Goodfellow (IT director): Purchasing and low-cost manufacturing	Role play: Choosing suppliers	Email
9	Logistics	Pull and push strategies; Supply-chaining (Thomas Friedman: The World Is Flat); Supply chain work flow	Alan Goodfellow: Inventory, Kanban and MRP; Leica's supply chain	Case study: Risk analysis	Summary; report

Map of the book

Unit		Reading	Listening	Speaking	Writing
10	Quality	Total Quality Management	Denis Frucot (hotel manager): Customer care and quality in a hotel	Role play: A hotel chain in trouble	Email
11	Products	Products and brands	Melissa Glass (juice bar director): Smoothies and a juice bar	Case study: Researching a product concept	Report
12	Marketing	The product life cycle; Marketing is everything (Regis McKenna: *Harvard Business Review*)	Melissa Glass: Promoting a juice bar	Case study: Promoting a new product	Description of distribution channels
13	Advertising	Advertising and viral marketing	Radio commercials	Scripting a radio commercial	Summaries; radio commercial
14	Banking	Banks and financial institutions; The subprime crisis and the credit crunch	Tony Ramos (HSBC): Commercial banking; Anna-Kim Hyun-Seung (expert on business ethics): Microfinance	Role play: Microfinance	Minutes of a meeting
15	Venture capital	A business plan	Chris Smart (venture capitalist): Investing in start-ups	Role play: Investing in start-ups	Summary
16	Bonds	Bonds; How to profit from bonds (*The Guardian* and *The Independent*)	Teresa La Thangue (Financial Services Authority): Bonds and subprime mortgages	Case study: Investing in funds	Report
17	Stocks and shares	Stocks and shares; Hedge funds (Geraint Anderson: *Cityboy*)	A financial news report (radio)	Role play: Investing a client's money	
18	Derivatives	Spread-betting (*Times Online*)	Teresa La Thangue: Hedge funds and structured products	Role play: Financial instruments	Training memo
19	Accounting and financial statements	Google Inc.'s financial statements	Richard Barker (senior lecturer in accounting): Valuing assets	Role play: Presenting a company's results	

Map of the book

Unit		Reading	Listening	Speaking	Writing
20	Market structure and competition	Market structure	Charles Cotton (IT consultant): Companies and clusters	Case study: Encouraging clusters	Briefing document
21	Takeovers	Takeovers, mergers and buyouts	Rory Taylor (Competition Commission): Market investigations	Role play: Is this company restricting competition?	Summary
22	Government and taxation	The role of government (Milton and Rose Friedman: *Free to Choose*)	Michael Kitson (senior lecturer in international macroeconomics): Government intervention	Presentation: Taxation and government spending	Presentation or report
23	The business cycle	What causes the business cycle?; Keynesianism and monetarism	Michael Kitson: Consumption and the business cycle; Keynesianism	Discussion: Government intervention	
24	Corporate social responsibility	Profits and social responsibility	Anna-Kim Hyun-Seung: Socially responsible investment; Stakeholder groups	Role play: Problems at a clothes manufacturer	Report
25	Efficiency and employment	Reorganizing the postal service	Anna-Kim Hyun-Seung: Efficiency, the number of employees, training and productivity	Role play: Reorganizing the postal service	Report
26	Exchange rates	Exchange rates	Michael Kitson: Currency flows and the Tobin Tax; Developing Africa	Case study: A currency transaction tax	Summary
27	International trade	Education and protection (Ha-Joon Chang, economist)	Michael Kitson: Free trade and exceptions	Presentation: For and against free trade	Presentation or report
28	Economics and ecology	The economics of climate change (Christian Gollier, economist)	Martin Beniston (professor of climate science): Climate policy	Role play: Recommending an energy policy	Summary

In the Student's Book only:

Role cards

Audio scripts

Appendix 1: How to give a good presentation

Appendix 2: Writing emails, letters and reports

List of role cards in the Student's Book

	Page in Student's Book
Unit 5 Role play: A job interview	
Assistant Brand Manager	143
Assistant Supply Chain Manager	143
Executive Assistant to the Chief Financial Officer	143
Interviewer	144
Unit 6 Role play: Do we need more women managers?	
CEO	145
Director A	147
Director B	149
Director C	151
Director D	153
Unit 10 Role play: A hotel chain in trouble	
CEO	145
Financial Director	147
Marketing Manager	149
Operations Manager	152
Unit 14 Role play: Microfinance	
Director A	145
Director B	148
Director C	150
Director D	152
Director E	153
Unit 18 Role play: Financial instruments	
Questions (1)	145
Questions (2)	148
Questions (3)	150

List of role cards in the Student's Book

Unit 21 Role play: Is this company restricting competition?
Investigator for the competition authority	146
Company manager A	148
Company manager B	150

Unit 24 Role play: Problems at a clothes manufacturer
CEO	146
Chief Scientist	149
Marketing Manager	151
Human Resources Manager	152
Financial Manager	154

Unit 25 Role play: Reorganizing the postal service
CEO	147
Financial Director	149
Human Resources Director	151
Trade Union Representative	153

Unit 28 Role play: Recommending an energy policy
Chairperson	154
Economist A	154
Economist B	154
Economist C	154

1 Management

This is the first of six units on management. It includes a listening activity about the qualities required by managers, based on the opinions of two MBA students at the Judge Business School of Cambridge University, a text summarizing the different functions of management as defined by the management theorist Peter Drucker, and a short communicative activity about recruiting the right manager.

Lead-in

These questions, like virtually all the questions, exercises and activities in the course, are to be discussed in pairs or small groups. The learners can then compare their answers with the rest of the class. (Unless you are teaching one-to-one, of course!)

Management is probably a mixture of innate qualities and learnable skills. Business schools clearly believe there are learnable skills and techniques, but they know that these alone do not suffice to make a great manager.

If the learners cannot think of business leaders they admire, you could perhaps suggest that they think of managers in *sport*: sports fans *all* have opinions about the managers of the teams they support.

Managers are figures of fun in many cultures. For example, in Britain, one of the most popular television comedy series in the early 2000s was *The Office*, featuring a disastrous manager acted (and co-written) by Ricky Gervais. The American cartoon strip *Dilbert*, which does nothing but ridicule managers, is also well known. In these countries there seems to be a widespread feeling that many managers have the unfortunate habit of making their subordinates' working lives unnecessarily difficult, by imposing too many procedures, meetings, performance reviews and appraisals, and so on.

The cartoon relates to a worry shared by many people lower down in hierarchies that their bosses unfairly get the credit and rewards for their subordinates' ideas.

Many learners are likely to choose Steve Jobs as the most interesting and impressive of the five managers shown, especially if they are the proud possessors of iPods and iPhones. His career path is certainly atypical. Akio Morita also had a remarkable career, and is an exemplary example of someone who understood inter-cultural differences. At the time of writing (early 2009), Carlos Ghosn (pronounced *Ghoson*) has had a remarkably successful career, and Meg Whitman's political career has yet to begin. Jack Welch is celebrated in business circles, but many people find his methods too ruthless: there are probably 10% of inefficient people in every 'un-Welched' organization; but firing 10% *every year*?

Listening: What makes a good manager? ▶1.2 ▶1.3

The Cambridge MBA students feature in the listening exercises in the first four units. Two of them have 'non-native' accents (Italian and Russian), while four of them speak established varieties of English, from India, Singapore and South Africa.

They speak quite quickly, so it will probably be necessary to play the recordings twice to let the learners answer the questions, and a third time to check their answers.

AUDIO SCRIPT

CARLO DE STEFANIS   ... so managers should pursue the company goal, maximize value for shareholders, and so on, but on the other hand they should accomplish also the personal goals and objective of the people they manage, for instance helping young professionals to develop, and understanding the expectation of everybody in their team, and trying to match goals of the company and even helping people to develop in their team.

OLGA BABAKINA   I believe that good managers actually don't manage anybody, and good managers basically they are good executors of strategies, because the companies today, those ones who are successful, are not those who have lots of business plans and strategies somewhere in the reports and files, but those companies who have managers, executors of plans, so basically in order to be a good manager you have to know how to lead people, how to motivate people, and how to make sure that you are meeting your targets ...

Management

ANSWERS

A good manager should:	Carlo	Olga
1 follow the company's goals	✓	
2 help subordinates to accomplish their own goals and objectives	✓	
3 help young colleagues to develop	✓	
4 know how to lead people	✓	✓
5 know how to motivate people		✓
6 make a maximum profit for the owners (the shareholders)	✓	
7 meet the targets they have been set		✓
8 successfully execute plans and strategies		✓

Discussion: What makes a good manager?

Other qualities that the learners may suggest include having good ideas, having integrity, being prepared to take risks and take responsibility for them, being hard-working, decisive, persuasive, honest, intelligent, educated, etc.

Reading: What is management?

A possible warm-up activity with the books closed, before reading the text: discuss in pairs for two minutes what exactly it is that managers *do*, hoping to elicit vague notions (though perhaps without the correct vocabulary) concerning organizing, setting objectives, allocating tasks and resources, communicating, motivating, budgeting, and so on.

Peter Drucker (1909–2005), the (Austrian-born) American management professor and consultant, was the author of many books about business. The text paraphrases the extended definition of management he gives in one of his management textbooks, *An Introductory View of Management* (1977).

ANSWERS

Among the qualities mentioned in the Listening, Drucker's first point (setting objectives and developing strategies) certainly involves following the company's goals. The second point (organizing) requires knowing how to lead people and knowing how to successfully execute plans and strategies. The third point (motivation and communication) again involves leading and developing people. The fourth point (measuring performance) involves meeting goals and targets. The fifth point (developing people) involves helping subordinates to accomplish their own goals and objectives and helping young colleagues to develop. But all this is clearly open to discussion.

Writing

The learners' written summaries are likely to be very similar to the sentences in the text.

Vocabulary

ANSWERS

1 1 D 2 E 3 B 4 F 5 H 6 G 7 A 8 C
2 1 set objectives 2 allocate, resources
  3 perform tasks 4 supervise, subordinates
  5 measure, performance 6 deal with crises, make, decisions

Vocabulary note

The plural of *crisis* is *crises*; cf. *thesis – theses, hypothesis – hypotheses*, and their pronunciation.

Case study: Selecting a Chief Operating Officer

This case study will not take long. (There is a longer exercise involving extracts from letters of application in **Unit 5** on Recruitment.)

> **SUGGESTED ANSWERS**
>
> Candidate 1 would appear to be the most suitable for Company C, which wants to maximize advertising revenue by broadcasting programmes with very large audiences. It wants its staff to execute senior management's strategies, and Candidate 1 has been successful at doing that.
>
> Candidate 2 would be suited to Company B, which has creative, talented and undisciplined people who need to be creative but probably also need to work in teams.
>
> Candidate 4 might be the best for Company A, which needs to implement new systems, and would also benefit from someone skilled at communicating with both employees and the outside world.
>
> Candidate 3 rather seems to see him or herself as a CEO setting objectives rather than a COO managing day-to-day operations, and is probably not best suited to the positions advertised.

Writing

> **MODEL ANSWER**
>
> I would recommend Candidate 4 for the position at Company A, which needs to implement new systems, and could use a skilful communicator. Candidate 2 would be suited to Company B, which needs to make its creative people work in teams. Candidate 1 is the most suitable for Company C, which needs its staff to execute senior management's strategies.

2 Work and motivation

As well as setting and communicating objectives, developing strategies and allocating resources, managers have to motivate the staff who report to them. These will often include people with interesting, responsible and fulfilling jobs, as well as others with less interesting and highly repetitive tasks. This unit contains discussion activities about the different factors that might motivate workers in both types of job, and about whether it can be argued that people in general like or dislike working. There are reading texts based on the work of two very well-known theorists of the psychology of work: Douglas McGregor, who put forward his Theories X and Y, and Frederick Herzberg, who distinguished between 'satisfiers', also referred to as 'hygiene factors', and 'motivators'. There is also (by popular demand, after its absence from the previous editions) a reference to Abraham Maslow's 'hierarchy of needs', with which business students tend to be very familiar. There are listening exercises based on interviews with four students from three different continents from the MBA programme at Cambridge University, talking about what factors can motivate different types of staff, based on their professional experience.

Lead-in

Encourage the learners to discuss these factors in pairs or groups before, during or after putting them in numerical order. You can then see if there is any consensus in a class discussion. Answers will probably depend on the age, maturity and work experience of the learners. Perhaps be prepared for not entirely friendly remarks about holidays (BrE) or vacations (AmE) and the teaching profession!

Other motivating factors could include having an interesting job (which is not the same as a challenging one), one that included a variety of tasks, one that required creativity, one that offered flexibility (of working hours, etc.), one that required all one's skills and experience, one that offered training, etc.

Discussion: Attitudes to work

As always, to be discussed in pairs. There are no 'right' answers, but these statements fall into two groups, reflecting two opposing views of human nature, as will be seen in the text that follows.

Reading: Theory X and Theory Y

ANSWERS
1 X   2 Y   3 X   4 X   5 Y   6 X   7 Y   8 Y

Notes

Douglas McGregor's *The Human Side of Enterprise* was published by McGraw-Hill in 1960. The diagram is adapted from Abraham Maslow's *Motivation and Personality* (first edition Harper, 1954; second edition Harper, 1970; third edition Addison-Wesley, 1987).

There is also a Theory Z, which was proposed by another American management theorist, William Ouchi, in 1981, based on the dominant Japanese management style at the time. Japanese companies often guaranteed long-term (even lifelong) employment, and were concerned with the employees' well-being; in return, workers could be expected to be loyal to the company, and to participate fully in decision making. Working relationships tended to be cooperative, with managers able to have a lot of trust in their staff, who were offered continuous training, and so became generalists rather than specialists. Ouchi argued that Theory Z management led to stable employment, high productivity, and high staff morale and satisfaction. Given that American companies do *not* usually guarantee long-term employment, however, Theory Z has had a limited impact in the US. The issue of 'labour market efficiency' and job security is the subject of **Unit 25**.

Comprehension

Learners can be asked to complete these sentences either orally (working in pairs), or in writing (alone or working in pairs).

> **SUGGESTED ANSWERS**
>
> 1 Because they are lazy and try to avoid work and responsibility
> 2 Because a responsible job is necessary to people's psychological well-being
> 3 Because there are people who are unable to take on responsibility and be self-disciplined

Writing

> **MODEL SUMMARIES**
>
> Theory X assumes that people are lazy and will avoid work and responsibility if they can, so workers have to be closely supervised and controlled, and told what to do. They have to be both threatened (e.g. with losing their job) and rewarded with financial incentives.
>
> Theory Y assumes that most people have a psychological need to work, are motivated by the satisfaction of doing a good job, are ambitious, and want to take responsibilities and be creative in their work.

Discussion

Learners who have *not* read the following text summarizing Frederick Herzberg's well-known argument that good working conditions merely *satisfy* but do not *motivate* workers, are likely to suggest improvements to working conditions as an answer to the second question.

Reading: 'Satisfiers' and 'motivators'

Herzberg first set out his ideas in *The Motivation to Work*, co-written with Bernard Mausner and Barbara Bloch Snyderman (Wiley, 1959; new edition Transaction, 1993). He developed them in *Work and the Nature of Man* (World Publishing Company, 1966), and further books in the 1980s.

Comprehension

> **ANSWERS**
>
> 1 False: he argued that they can only satisfy or dissatisfy, but not motivate
> 2 False: they are motivators
> 3 True
> 4 True
> 5 True
> 6 False: not all companies can be the best in their field

Vocabulary

> **ANSWERS**
>
> 1 labour relations 2 job security 3 wages
> 4 benefits 5 incentives 6 promotion
> 7 unskilled 8 job rotation 9 corporate culture

Vocabulary notes

Other expressions for non-cash *benefits* are *perks* (short for *perquisites*) and *fringe benefits*.

The term *labour relations* usually applies to industries in which there is a history of conflicts between management or owners and the labour force, often organized in *trade unions* (BrE) or *labor unions* (AmE). People with comfortable professional jobs often talk about the atmosphere or ambience at work.

Wages is commonly used for factory jobs and casual employment; people with regular jobs get *salaries*.

Discussion

Herzberg's theory is not universally accepted. There are many managers who believe that what Herzberg called 'hygiene factors' *do* motivate staff (including the Marks & Spencer manager in the first two editions of this course).

Listening 1: Managers and motivation
▶ 1.4

As mentioned in **Unit 1**, some of the Cambridge MBA students speak rather quickly. They also have distinctive accents, revealing where they come from. You will probably need to play the recordings twice, and if necessary a third time with the learners reading from the audio scripts at the back of the Student's Book. You should discourage them from reading these before you specifically invite them to.

Management

AUDIO SCRIPT

KRISHNA SRINIVASAN I would say that coming from an auditing world where the pays are typically really low, especially when compared to the banking guys, one of the core things that was a driver in retaining our staff was, I would say, problems. The more you give them challenging problems, and the more you make them excited about solving the problem, the monetary aspect just goes out of the picture, and I have seen staff who have been almost telling every day that they want to quit the firm, but have never quit the firm for the last seven years, just because they've had so many challenging problems, that they just enjoyed solving, and you ask them, 'Why didn't you move, given that you would have had such a high pay increase in another place?' They'd say, 'Well, the pay would be great, but I don't think I'll face as many challenging puzzles or whatever problems I solved here over there.' So I think the motivation of the mind or the ultimate passion that you have is still a core driver, no matter how many hygiene factors or whatever that you learn in motivation.

CARLO DE STEFANIS Managers can make the difference from this point of view. I think it is hard to engage people just setting up or devising a set of rules or a set of incentives to motivate people. Statistics in a way say that when people leave a company they leave their boss first. So really, it's about a balance of being a manager and being leader, having a vision, inspiring other people, helping them to develop that can get them engaged, I think.

SAKTIANDI SUPAAT Something just came up about motivation, if I may raise the point ... Talking about managers that can motivate somebody, another additional point that I thought useful to bring up is a manager which is influential, and knows how to be an intermediary between the senior management and his staff, can motivate the staff, because he knows what the organization wants, and he's influential enough to convince the organization to do things that the staff wants. So having a manager that is influential and able to actually influence the organization is I think a great motivator, I mean from my perspective.

Notes

Krishna uses *pays* in the plural, which is less common than the uncountable *pay*, and *telling* where *saying* would be more standard. He twice uses the word *core*, meaning central or very important, once in the expression *core drivers* – the most important things that motivate someone to do something.

ANSWERS

1 Krishna says that pay is really low, compared to banking.
2 By offering them challenging problems or puzzles to solve
3 Because they are not satisfied with their boss
4 Carlo says that they are not enough to motivate people ('it is hard to engage people just setting up or devising a set of rules or a set of incentives to motivate people'), but he does not say they are unnecessary.
5 He says the manager must also be a leader, have a vision, and inspire people, and help them to develop.
6 Saktiandi says that a manager who is influential, and who is a good intermediary between the senior management and his staff, 'can convince the organization to do things that the staff wants.' (In other words, he suggests that the organization should do what the staff want.)
7 He says that having a manager who can influence the organization and convince it to do things that the staff want is very motivating for the staff.

Discussion

There are clearly no 'right answers' here. Pre-service learners may not yet be able to say truthfully whether they would stay in a fascinating but low-paid job. Similarly, they may not know whether working for someone influential in an organization would be motivating. I don't know how true it is that dissatisfaction with one's boss is the 'first' reason for leaving a company. Carlo hedges his statement by saying 'Statistics *in a way* say ...'

Listening 2: Out-of-work activities
▶ 1.5

AUDIO SCRIPT

JANINE GEORGE I had a few team members in my operational team who were working in their jobs for about 40 years. It was a detergent factory, they came in every single day for 12-hour shifts, and can you imagine working in that role for 40 years? I came in and people were really bored, right, and what I did is, we set up small group meetings for each of the shifts, right, to find out what sports they were interested in, right, and what things they were doing outside of work. I found that there were many entrepreneurs, and also other people interested in things like driving HIV/Aids activities – in South Africa that's quite a big problem at the moment. And I just mean outside of work. I mean, if it's reading a book, if it's kicking a soccer ball, perhaps they want to organize a staff soccer team, right, perhaps they want to start a book club inside work, and I'm not just talking about, and I'm talking about things outside of things related to the bottom line, and I feel that those things could make people more passionate, just about coming into work, getting up in the morning and coming to their jobs. People then wanted to be trained, and what we found is they were even willing to come in on the off-shifts, and even not get paid for these types of things. So I think the one thing you need to learn about motivation is how do you ensure that you mobilize people by finding out what they really enjoy doing and you need to be extremely creative about these things. And I think it relates in some ways very much to jobs that secretaries do. People think that they're OK with just sitting behind a desk, and organizing your inbox, and sending out meeting requests. They're *not*, so I think it's really up to these managers and leaders to become creative, understand their people, and really think about things – and I don't want to use this word – outside of the box, to try and motivate their staff.

ANSWERS

1. 40 years
2. A detergent factory
3. They do 12-hour shifts.
4. Bored
5. She set up meetings to find out what they were interested in outside of work.
6. She found that some were entrepreneurs and others were involved in helping people with HIV/Aids.
7. Reading books, playing football
8. You need to find out about your staff and be very creative when coming up with ideas for motivating people.
9. The 'bottom line' is usually the last line on a profit and loss account or income statement, showing 'net income'. (See **Unit 17**.) 'Outside of things related to the bottom line' means things that do not directly contribute to making a profit, or which even cost the company money, but which might make the staff more motivated (even 'more passionate') about their jobs.
10. 'Thinking outside (of) the box' means thinking unconventionally, from a new or different perspective. This expression has become a cliché in business, widely used (or overused) by consultants, which is probably why Janine says she doesn't want to use it.

Note

In fact the bottom line is often not the last line on a profit and loss account or income statement, because accountants have devised various 'below the line items' (such as out-of-the-ordinary or non-recurring revenues or charges). Analysing below the line items might be one of the challenging puzzles or problems that Krishna talks about!

Management

Case study: A car manufacturer

There are no 'right answers', but here are some subjective remarks.

Subsidizing the staff canteen would probably please everybody. It would be relatively inexpensive, and most people enjoy getting something for nothing, or cheaply. The senior management would probably choose to subsidize their company restaurant too!

Similarly, offering cars at discount prices would probably be well received by everybody. If the sales reps don't already have free company cars, giving them one would be another possibility.

Career training would almost certainly be appreciated by designers and secretarial and administrative staff.

Paying higher salaries would probably please everybody too, but this is usually an unrealistic suggestion. Reducing the working week and offering early retirement are also generally prohibitively expensive.

Establishing profit-sharing programmes isn't easy, as profits legally belong to the shareholders. It would involve distributing shares to staff, but the possible gains would be minimal compared to an annual salary, unless everyone was given a huge quantity of stock options, a perk which is usually reserved for very senior managers.

Paying productivity bonuses can be dangerous, as it tends to run counter to a concern with quality (see **Unit 10**).

Setting up a crèche for employees' pre-school-age children might well be popular with all groups of staff, as might building sports facilities, though neither of these options would come cheap. Decorating the organization's premises is clearly what Herzberg would call a hygiene factor, not a motivator.

Giving longer paid holidays to long-term staff would almost certainly be very well received by production-line workers, cleaners and canteen and restaurant staff.

Writing

> **MODEL ANSWER**
>
> The senior management recently met to discuss possible ways of increasing staff motivation.
>
> We would like to suggest the following relatively inexpensive measures:
> - Subsidizing the staff canteen, which would probably please all categories of staff.
> - Offering a discount on our cars to all categories of staff.
> - Offering more career training to the designers and the secretarial and administrative staff.
> - Spending more money on office decoration (plants, pictures, etc.).
> - Investigating the possibility of setting up a crèche for employees' pre-school-age children.
>
> We will shortly be submitting a full report.

See also the role play 'Extra perks' in *Business Roles 2* by John Crowther-Alwyn (Cambridge University Press).

3 Company structure

One of the most important tasks for the management of any organization employing more than a few people is to determine its organizational structure, and to change this when and where necessary. This unit contains a text about 'wikinomics' and another outlining the most common traditional organizational systems, an exercise focusing on the potential conflicts between the different departments of a manufacturing organization, and listening and discussion activities concerning the advantages and disadvantages of working in big and small companies.

Lead-in

Learners who are working or have previously worked will probably have more to say than full-time students, but the latter should at least know what they want to do and why. In-service learners may know more about how easy it is to change departments during the course of a career.

Here is an **additional question**: Would you like to work independently, as a freelance or an expert or a consultant, rather than work for an organization?

Reading: Wikinomics and the future of companies

The answer to the pre-reading question is that more and more work is being outsourced from companies to independent suppliers.

There are no further comprehension or vocabulary questions with this text, as the first paragraph consists largely of definitions, and the rest of the vocabulary is quite straightforward.

Potential disadvantages of wikinomics include the fact that it might not work (!), and that advertising your needs probably alerts competitors to your plans.

Learners could be given a week to come up with 'wikinomic' suggestions.

Vocabulary

> ANSWERS
>
> **1** hierarchy or chain of command   **2** function
> **3** autonomous   **4** line authority   **5** to report to
> **6** to delegate

Reading: Company structure

The text summarizes the most common ways in which companies and other organizations are structured, and mentions the more recent development of matrix management, and a well-known objection to it.

If you think the learners may already know about company organization, the text can also be prepared orally by way of questions such as the following (each of which presupposes an answer to the previous one):

- How are most organizations structured?
- Most companies are too large to be organized as a single hierarchy. The hierarchy is usually divided up. In what way?
- What are the obvious disadvantages of functional organization?
- *(Discuss briefly in pairs.)* Give some examples of standard conflicts of interest between departments with different objectives.
- Are there any other ways of organizing companies that might solve these problems?

> SUGGESTED ANSWERS
>
> - Hierarchies have a clear chain of command, so everybody knows what decisions they are able to make, and who their superiors and their immediate subordinates are. But people at lower levels are unable to make important decisions, and have to pass on responsibility to their boss.
> - Specialized functional departments are generally efficient, but people sometimes feel a responsibility to their department rather than to the company as a whole. People in functional departments are unlikely to think of innovations concerning the whole company.

Unit 3 Company structure

Management

- Matrix management allows people to report to more than one superior, without passing everything through their line superior. But matrices involving several departments can become quite complex.
- Projects can be carried out by autonomous, temporary teams, but teams are not always very good at decision making, and usually require a strong leader.

Comprehension

ANSWERS

1 Everyone knows what decisions they are able to make, and who they can give instructions to.
2 Because their activities are too complicated
3 People may be more concerned about the success of their department than that of the company.
4 The desire to save money and make decision making easier; the use of IT (information technology) systems; and the need to reduce costs during a recession
5 The owners of small businesses, because they want to control as much as possible
6 They can become quite complex, making decision making difficult.
7 If they do not have a strong leader, and need to make a lot of decisions

Vocabulary

ANSWERS

The following word combinations or collocations are in the text:
- delegate decision making
- delegate responsibilities
- give instructions
- give priority
- make decisions
- motivate staff
- take decisions.

Other collocations are also possible, e.g. 'take responsibility' is also common.

Pronunciation note

With advanced classes, it might be worth mentioning that the verb *delegate* is pronounced /ˈdelɪgeɪt/ with a long vowel in the *–ate* (like *motivate*), whereas the noun *delegate* (a person chosen or elected by a group to speak or vote for them at a meeting) is pronounced /ˈdelɪgət/. Cf. the verbs and nouns *advocate, associate, duplicate, estimate, graduate, moderate*, and the verbs and adjectives *alternate, animate, appropriate, approximate, articulate, deliberate, elaborate, intimate, legitimate, moderate, separate*, etc.

Discussion: Incompatible goals

MODEL ANSWER

1, 4 and 11 would logically satisfy production managers, although 11 should also satisfy other departments.

2, 3, 6, 7 and 9 would logically be the demands of marketing managers.

5, 8, 10 and 12 would logically keep finance managers happy.

Note

This exercise might be difficult for less advanced classes as it includes a number of words that are not defined here or practised elsewhere in the unit (but which recur in later units: e.g. *capacity, credit facilities, features, inventory, market share, retained earnings, sales force*).

Listening: Big and small companies

▶ 1.6

AUDIO SCRIPT

KRISHNA SRINIVASAN I guess given the way we are, or the way I am, it actually doesn't matter whether I'm in a big or a small company. What matters is, who am I going to work with? So if I have five people who are probably extremely different, or extremely similar, at the end of the day, as long as I enjoy working with them, and the basic security of supporting your family is assured, it doesn't matter which company I'm in. Problems, nice people – it doesn't matter anything else.

CARLO DE STEFANIS I dare say it's, big company or a small company, it depends at what stage even you are in your career. For instance, should I give an advice I dare say for somebody who has just left university, working for a while in a big company can be a very good opportunity because they will form you, you will learn what are the best practices in the sector. But probably after a few years – I don't know, four or five years – everybody has to find his own way, because they think that they … in my opinion, big companies and small and medium enterprises are quite different in their mentality. In big companies, probably, politics can be more important, because you are actually a number within, you know, a large pool of people, it's hard to differentiate. In a smaller company maybe it's more a hands-on approach where you have more, it's required more an entrepreneurial style, so I think that everybody has to find his own way according to his liking basically.

OLGA BABAKINA For me the size of the company doesn't really matter. Most important is the culture, so even if you are a small company or a big company, if you don't have the shared values with your colleagues, or if nobody understands what is the company's culture, nobody has a common vision, then it doesn't really matter. So the most important is the culture, and that everyone in the organization understands what the company is trying to achieve over the short term, over the long term, and everyone shares the same corporate values. Of course small companies have more challenges in proving themselves as successful businesses. Big corporations, of course, on the other hand, are not that flexible, so it's more difficult for them to adopt new changes, and maybe to incorporate some creativity and innovation, so a balance in between all those issues, I think, is the key.

> **SUGGESTED ANSWERS**
>
> 1 Because the important thing is his colleagues ('nice people'), and whether the job is interesting (and gives him problems to solve). He also says 'the basic security of supporting your family' is important.
> 2 Because they will train you (he says 'form you'), and you will learn about the best practices in the sector
> 3 He says that in a big company with a large pool of people, it's hard to differentiate yourself, so you might have to engage in office politics. In a small company, you might have to do more, and have a 'more hands-on approach' and a more 'entrepreneurial style'.
> 4 The company's culture or shared corporate values or common vision
> 5 She says big corporations are less flexible, so it's difficult for them to adopt new changes or be creative and innovative.

Discussion: Big and small companies

Discussion of the second and third questions here might cover some of the ten statements in the Student's Book – especially if the learners are looking at them!

> **ANSWERS**
>
> Advantages of working in a small company: 1, 2, 3, 7, 8
>
> Advantages of working in a big company: 4, 5, 6, 9, 10

Presentation

These short (3–5 minute) presentations can either be prepared in class or as homework. They should be restricted to the points mentioned: what the organization does, where it is located, how it is structured and whether the structure contributes to its success, and if it is not the learner's current employer, what it is about this organization that makes them want to work for it.

In large classes the presentations could be made to groups rather than the whole class.

4 Managing across cultures

Despite the growth of global brands, and some degree of convergence of consumer tastes and habits, there remain enormous cultural differences among different countries and continents. This clearly presents a dilemma to multinational corporations: should they attempt to export their management methods to all their subsidiaries, or should they adapt their methods to the local culture in each country or continent? This unit contains listening exercises based on the opinions of MBA students from three continents, a text that describes cultures in different parts of the world (according to the intercultural theorist Richard D. Lewis), and several discussion and writing activities about cultural attitudes.

Here is some background information, summarizing the work of the best-known intercultural theorists.

BACKGROUND INFORMATION

Despite many people's multicultural and bi- or multilingual reality, in these days of increasing migration and mobility, the major intercultural theorists tend to describe 'national cultural characteristics'. They all have their own models of the dimensions or characteristics or determinants of national cultures.

For example, the American theorist Edward T. Hall divides the world into high-context and low-context cultures. High-context cultures – the norm in East Asia – are 'affiliation cultures' in which people tend to have similar experiences and expectations, allowing many things to be left unsaid. In high-context communication people rely more on non-verbal communication (facial expression, gestures, eye movement) and inferences that can be drawn from implicit shared cultural knowledge. People in such cultures are said to have a greater ability to anticipate and understand the feelings of others than in low-context cultures. Low-context cultures often consist of people with a wider variety of backgrounds, so in low-context communication – the norm in Europe and North America – people use more direct or explicit verbal communication, and are said to be less adept at interpreting non-verbal and emotional clues.

Whereas Hall divides the world into two types of cultures, Geert Hofstede distinguishes three levels of 'human mental programming'. Between the universal level (determined by biology and physiology) and the individual level (the realm of psychology) comes a collective level – patterns of thinking, feeling and acting, and values (or mental programmes) that everyone in a particular cultural context acquires in childhood socialization and carries through life, which are resilient to change and often contain strong national components that are passed on from generation to generation.

Hofstede outlines four bi-polar dimensions of national culture, three of which are self-explanatory: 'individualism vs collectivism', 'masculinity vs femininity', and 'uncertainty avoidance'. The fourth is 'power distance' – the extent to which the less powerful members of institutions and organizations expect and accept that power is distributed unequally.

Fons Trompenaars, another influential Dutch theorist, outlines seven aspects of national cultures: 'universalism' vs 'particularism' (discussed in the reading text in this unit); 'individualism vs communitarianism'; 'specific vs diffuse' approaches to business relationships – whether people stick to facts and data, or use feelings and goodwill; 'neutrality vs affectivity' – whether people control their emotions in professional contexts, or show their emotions and become involved; 'inner-directed vs outer-directed attitude' – whether or not people believe they can control and direct their environment; 'achieved status vs ascribed status' – whether you are judged on what you have accomplished, or whether status is ascribed to you according to birth, kinship, gender, age, rank or connections; and 'sequential time vs synchronic time'.

Hall, Hofstede and Trompenaars are the most widely cited theorists, but there are many others. Shalom Schwartz proposes an alternative set of dimensions – embeddedness vs intellectual and affective autonomy, hierarchy vs egalitarianism, and mastery vs harmony, while Ronald Inglehart classifies countries according to two dimensions – traditional vs secular-rational values and survival vs self-expression values.

Most of this work is based on questionnaire research, largely concerning the attitudes of businesspeople to workplace issues, and Hofstede's data (admittedly well over 100,000 questionnaires) comes from a single multinational company, IBM. This leads to the common criticism that such research only shows what a country's culture would be like if everybody in it worked for IBM – imagine questionnaire results based entirely on language teachers! – but the researchers obviously claim that such data is more reliable than simple observation.

See:
Edward T. Hall, *Beyond Culture* (New York: Anchor Press, 1976).
Geert Hofstede, *Culture's Consequences: Comparing Values, Behaviors, Institutions and Organizations Across Nations* Second Edition (Thousand Oaks CA: Sage Publications, 2001).
Geert Hofstede, *Cultures and Organization: Software of the Mind* (London: McGraw-Hill, 1991).
Ronald Inglehart, *Modernization and Postmodernization: Cultural, Economic, and Political Change in 43 Societies* (Princeton: Princeton University Press, 1997).
Shalom H. Schwartz, 'Mapping and interpreting cultural differences around the world', in *Comparing Cultures, Dimensions of Culture in a Comparative Perspective.* Eds H. Vinken, J. Soeters, and P. Ester (Leiden: Brill, 2004).
Fons Trompenaars and Charles Hampden-Turner, *Riding the Waves of Culture: Understanding Cultural Diversity in Business.* Second Edition (London: Nicholas Brealey, 1997).

Lead-in

It is generally agreed that it is more efficient for multinational companies to adapt their methods to the local cultures in which their subsidiaries are situated.

Listening 1: Managers and authority
▶ 1.7

AUDIO SCRIPT

KRISHNA SRINIVASAN What I noticed in – I worked in both in Switzerland and in Malaysia – and the context of a manager is very different in these two countries. In Singapore the emphasis on hierarchy and the superiority of the manager is very important. No matter you put a group in a team, once the manager says something it's kind of accepted by everyone else, no one challenges it, whereas in Switzerland and UK what you observe is once the manager says something, people can challenge him. So manager in the western context is more a guider, who encourages people by his persuasion, either his vocal talent or his technical attitude [astute], whereas in the Asian region I still feel that the emphasis on superiority, power, is still very prevalent, so the manager has to have the commanding power.

CARLO DE STEFANIS My theory in Italy we've still got, authority is important, as is seniority, in respect – if I make a comparison especially with the Anglo-Saxon world, in Italy seniority, the years you have spent in a certain position, in a certain company, give you formal authority, in a way. On the other hand I think that it is accepted, largely accepted in Italy, to make your point with your boss, absolutely, so to discuss about a position and problems in an open way.

ANSWERS

1 Hierarchy, the superiority of the manager, and power
2 In Europe, people can challenge their managers, who have to guide, encourage and persuade their subordinates.
3 Carlo says that in Italy authority, seniority and respect are still important. You can 'make your point with your boss', but not 'challenge' him or her. Italy is more like Singapore than the UK or Switzerland.

Notes

Respect for seniority is more common in Latin and Asian cultures than North American and northern European ones. Similarly, there is more possibility for a dynamic, young manager to rise quickly in the hierarchy in, say, the USA, Canada, Britain and Scandinavia than in Italy, Spain, Argentina, Japan or India.

Reading: Managing across cultures

This text is based on Richard D. Lewis's model of cultural types, as outlined in his book *The Cultural Imperative: Global Trends in the 21st Century* (Yarmouth, MN: Intercultural Press, 2003). The diagram is based on the one on the back cover of this book.

Management

Comprehension

ANSWERS

1 Because local cultural habits, beliefs and principles can easily affect the performance of their business in each country
2 An individualist is someone who believes that personal goals and desires and interests are more important than those of a group of people; a collectivist is someone who believes in the importance of a group of people rather than separate individuals.
3 People in reactive cultures
4 Universalists
5 Particularists

Vocabulary

ANSWERS

1 glocalization 2 logic 3 confrontation
4 compromise 5 intuition 6 connections
7 improvise 8 status 9 collectivist
10 lose face 11 interrupt 12 eye contact

Discussion: Managing across cultures

ANSWERS AND NOTES

1 There is no 'right answer' to this question. Intercultural trainers clearly believe that you can sum up national characteristics in a few words, and that there is some truth in stereotypes.
2–4 See the map on Richard Lewis's website: http://www.crossculture.com/publications/maps/ (consulted January 2009).
5a This is more likely to work in linear-active cultures, in which people tend to be individualistic, rather than collectivist. In *Riding the Waves of Culture*, Trompenaars gives the anecdote of a sales rep in an Italian subsidiary of a US multinational who was given a huge quarterly bonus under a new policy imposed by head office. His sales – which had been high for years – declined dramatically during the following three months. It was later discovered that he was deliberately not selling more than his colleagues, and was desperate not to earn more than his boss, as this would obviously humiliate him. Trompenaars also reports that Singaporean and Indonesian managers thought that pay-for-performance caused salesmen to pressure customers into buying products they didn't really need, which was not only bad for long-term business relations, but quite simply unfair and ethically wrong.
b This seems to work for service industry jobs in the US (hotels, fast-food restaurants, etc.). It is often laughed at in northern Europe, and is unlikely to work in collectivist cultures.
c Matrix management is more efficient in linear-active cultures. In multi-active and reactive cultures, in which status and hierarchy are important, the (task-oriented) logic of matrix management conflicts with the principle of loyalty to one's important line superior, or functional boss.
d Teamwork is increasingly common even in 'individualist' countries. However, teams are not always very good for decision making, and they run the risk of relational problems, unless they are small and have a lot of self-discipline. Even in individualist cultures, teams still require a definite leader, on whom their success probably depends.

Writing: You and your influences

As with various other exercises in the Student's Book, you may feel that too much information is given here. If you would prefer your learners to suggest these possible influences themselves, rather than merely select from a list, you could do a version of this exercise as a discussion, with the students' books closed. They could then do the writing exercise, choosing five factors and putting them in order. There are clearly no 'right answers' here.

> **MODEL ANSWER**
>
> I think my genes or DNA are the most important influence, because these are inherited characteristics that you can't change. I think early family environment is also important, even if its influence is unconscious. I expect that I also have a lot of characteristics that are considered typical of my country, which I cannot change. I think I am consciously influenced by my friends and social life, the things I choose to do in my free time. In fifth place I'd put higher education; I think my university and what I studied there had a big effect on me.

Listening 2: Managers and cultural diversity ▶ 1.8

AUDIO SCRIPT

LAKSHMI JAYA I mean I think here diversity in, say, management schools plays a very important role, because take for example Judge Business School, we have people from forty-six different nationalities, so you're working with these group of people at various points through your programme, and it kind of like gives that diverse experience to you, to be able to like work with cross, people from cross-cultural backgrounds. So I think management education does help a lot, and your ability to be, work with like, cross-cultural people.

JANINE GEORGE I think the difference nowadays is also the fact that there's a lot more awareness about these issues. The fact that there are so many business schools, so many courses running with regards to culture, the differences in aspects regarding the US versus China, and so forth, people are just more aware. And I think with this, an American now going into China, has a completely different attitude, or at least I hope so! That people are now more aware of these situations and sort of aspects of emotional intelligence allow people to use those self-awareness aspects, to be able to be a bit more effective in their management styles …

CARLO DE STEFANIS I read somewhere that now there are a lot of international corporations that are giving up their passport. This was an article, I mean, about a more general context, but it's true that companies like IBM, or General Electric, that are moving a lot of executives, and even middle management across the countries, contribute to create a mutual understanding of different cultures and to smooth, in a way, to round the corners, I think.

JANINE GEORGE There's a saying that says 'When in Rome, do as the Romans do.' I went on a Japanese course where it said, 'When in Rome, learn what the Romans do, so you can become a better Japanese.' So I think that in a way sums it up perfectly, in that culture will never disappear, right, but I think in a way we're just going to become a lot more profound in what we do, and learn a lot more what everybody else in the rest of the world is doing.

> **ANSWERS**
>
> 1 The diversity of the students, which gives you experience in working with people from different cultural backgrounds
> 2 Because there are so many business schools and so many courses on culture
> 3 Emotional intelligence (this is the ability to understand and manage your own emotions, and to understand other people's)
> 4 He says they 'are giving up their passport'.
> 5 This helps create a mutual understanding of different cultures, and to make the differences smaller ('to smooth … to round the corners').
> 6 'When in Rome, do as the Romans do.' This means that when in another country, you should try to adopt local ways of behaving.
> 7 'When in Rome, learn what the Romans do, so you can become a better Japanese.' This means that a good Japanese (or any other business traveller) should learn how to behave appropriately in other countries.

Management

Role play: Welcoming American colleagues

After the groups discuss and present to the class what they think should go in this document, they could also write the document (perhaps collectively, in pairs or groups).

Additional discussion questions

Here are some additional discussion questions about corporate culture and body language. These exercises would probably work better with mixed classes containing learners of different languages, nationalities and cultures. If you have a homogeneous class, you could try to get them to suggest which countries or cultures might have motivated some of these questions (e.g. Japanese culture has very strict conventions about making eye contact; blowing one's nose in public is considered impolite in many east Asian countries, etc.).

In your company, or in your country in general, is it acceptable to:
- show that you are emotionally involved in your work?
- make eye contact with hierarchical superiors?
- wear fairly casual clothes to work?
- make jokes in meetings?
- disagree with superiors in meetings?
- occasionally arrive late for work or meetings?
- socialize with superiors and/or subordinates?

In your country or culture, is it considered acceptable to:
- gesticulate (make hand and arm movements) while you talk?
- move very close to someone as you talk to them?
- touch someone on the arm as you speak to them?
- blow your nose in public?
- look at someone in the eyes for a long time while talking to them?
- look at someone in the eyes for a long time while they are talking to you?
- laugh loudly at work, and in meetings?

> See also the role plays 'Flexible working time' in *Business Roles* and 'No Smoking' in *Business Roles 2* by John Crowther-Alwyn, and the simulation 'The barbecue' in *Decisionmaker* by David Evans (Cambridge University Press).

5 Recruitment

This unit considers the process by which companies and other organizations recruit new members of staff, and discusses what kind of information given on a curriculum vitae or resume might help a job applicant to be selected for an interview. There is a model of a curriculum vitae and a skeleton of a covering letter (or cover letter), and advice about writing job applications (letters and CVs) and doing job interviews. There is a listening activity about job interviews and the psychology of interviewers, and a role play involving a job interview.

Lead-in

- It depends on who you talk to, but I have heard HR people say that for junior jobs, they spend less than a minute per CV, and sometimes much less.
- Replies to questionnaires I sent to leading employers of business graduates in continental Europe revealed that what they like most is professional experience. Relevant experience is, of course, the most desirable, but not everyone has the possibility to do traineeships or internships. Failing that, work experience of any kind is a definite advantage.
- There's no knowing how many times today's students will change jobs during their career, but the long-term trend is towards more mobility. There is of course no fixed correlation between the number of positions people apply for and the number of times they change jobs.

The **cartoon** is supposed to be amusing rather than dispiriting! But big employers *do* receive large quantities of CVs or resumes. The cartoon dates from the early 1990s; these days *resume* is often spelled without the acute accents.

Reading: Filling a vacancy

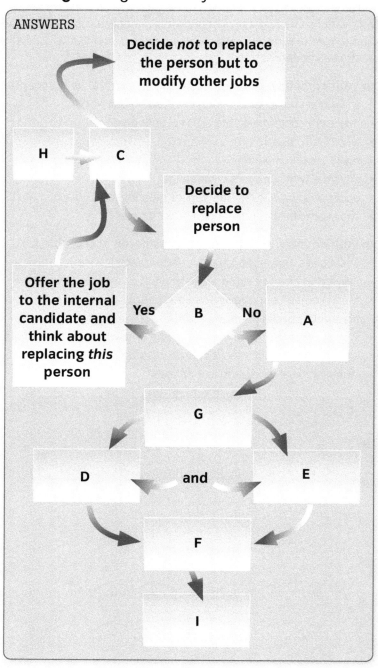

28   Unit 5 Recruitment

Management

It will be seen from this chart that the order of D and E could easily be reversed (i.e. some companies prefer to interview candidates personally before asking for references about them). If someone has been in a particular job for several years, the only reference that is really useful is his/her current employer's reference, but companies do not usually ask for these for candidates who are unlikely to be given the job.

Obviously, an employer should not reject all the other candidates until the selected candidate has agreed to take the job. (Other non-shortlisted candidates could, of course, have been rejected at an earlier stage, simultaneously with D or E.)

Vocabulary notes

Americans generally use *resume/résumé*, a word of French origin, rather than *curriculum vitae*, but of course the verb to *resume* in English does not mean to summarize, as in French, but to begin again or continue after an interruption.

The plural of *curriculum vitae* is *curricula vitae*.

Reading and discussion: Job applications

> POSSIBLE (SUBJECTIVE) ANSWERS
>
> As mentioned above, in the notes to the **Lead-in**, employers' first criterion is generally professional experience. This is, of course, problematic for a first job, but any work experience of any kind is a definite advantage. Even if you have only spent three weeks during a summer holiday filling the shelves in a supermarket it *is* work experience, and demonstrates that you can get up and go to work every day for three weeks. Consequently extract **5**, which shows someone who has regularly worked at weekends and during college vacations, is good for any application. Some students may object to the way extract **5** is written, and suggest writing 'stock management' instead of 'shelf-filling'; I am unconvinced.
>
> Extract **7** is similar to many models given for American covering letters. It may appear to some to be over-confident ('excellent match', 'experience', 'communication skills', 'increasing your sales volume') but this kind of thing is fairly standard in American job applications, particularly for sales positions, as is the sentence in extract **2** about 'how I can benefit your company'. Extract **1** also vaunts skills and experience, but job applications need to have a positive tone and content.
>
> Languages are usually an advantage for international business, although it depends on the job and the country. The languages listed in extract **4** would almost certainly be an advantage for a job with international responsibilities (provided that the claims made were true).
>
> For a job that involves working closely with other people, evidence of having been a successful team member, as in extract **3**, is generally an advantage. But being a successful individual performer in sport, music, etc. also shows commitment, determination, self-discipline, and so on. Apart from sports and hobbies, work in student associations, etc., is usually well thought of.
>
> Many companies are suspicious of people who seem only to have studied, and prefer people with a wide range of experience and interests to those with brilliant exam results but nothing else. But it depends on the job: finance and R&D might require more evidence of brains than, say, jobs in selling (though this is a subject for discussion). Many learners are prejudiced against those who get very high exam results, and may scoff at extract **9**. If they do, ask them how they feel about using a doctor, dentist, lawyer, architect or engineer who may have passed his/her degree with a mark of only 60%, i.e. getting 40% wrong! Many employers expect to find a correlation between the amount of time and effort devoted to study and exam results. Hence low marks should be justified by extra-curricular activities.
>
> Travel, we say, broadens the mind, but if you've only ever travelled and never had a holiday job it doesn't look good. Extract **6** is supposed to be a parody, but there seems to be one learner per class who selects it as the best!
>
> American culture seems to require more self-confidence than in much of Europe or Asia, but there remains a distinction between self-confidence and arrogance. 'Your company would have a great deal to gain from employing me' is way over the top.
>
> Extract **8** is even more appalling. The first sentence is empty, and far too generalized. It should be more targeted and specific, mentioning the type

of position and company sought. The list of attributes the candidate is claiming is also empty and fairly meaningless, e.g. no organization will want to employ a person who *isn't* 'results orientated'; no one is going to apply for a job and claim *not* to be 'a team player' or to 'work well in a team'. Someone just graduating from college is unlikely to have much 'project management' and 'people management' experience. General statements such as these should be backed up with facts or examples, so someone who *does* have experience should add details (e.g. 'I used my communication skills to …', 'I led a team which …', 'I organized a …', 'I managed a budget of €100,000', etc.). Although employers probably *are* looking for commitment, creativity, a competitive spirit, ambition, adaptability, flexibility, etc., just listing these qualities without giving any examples, or demonstrations that one possesses these qualities, is a waste of time. Similarly, an applicant should indicate where and how he/she has met deadlines, analysed and solved problems, made decisions, and found solutions and implemented them.

Notes on CVs/resumes and covering letters

For detailed advice and information about CVs, letters, job interviews, following up job interviews, etc., see Colm Downes, *Cambridge English for Job-hunting*.

The notes on CVs/resumes and covering letters do not come with tasks or exercises; they simply present advice for learners. There are Discussion questions with the model CV and covering letter below.

An anecdote to reinforce the point about correct spelling: during my (successful) interview for my first summer teaching job, the Principal of the language school showed me three applications lying unopened on his desk, in envelopes addressed to 'The Principle'.

The example CV in the Student's Book is just one way of writing one. Consequently learners may say that they would present their CV differently in their own language. Many other styles, and actual examples, can be found by doing a web search for 'sample resumes'.

The outline covering letter is the kind of thing that a university student might write. Or at least a modest British student; American letters and resumes are often more direct and even boastful, but I am incapable of even imitating one! There are examples in *Cambridge English for Job-hunting*. Your learners may well insist that their covering letters would be more assertive in outlining their talents.

It should be mentioned that the models given here are only indicative of British and American writing styles; other varieties of English (or other 'World Englishes') in Asia and Africa can have very different writing styles.

An obvious **Writing** task would be to have the learners write a CV – though if they are first-year students without much in the way of qualifications or work experience, they may prefer to wait a couple of years. On the other hand, a CV is requested in the Role play which follows.

Discussion: CVs/resumes and covering letters

SUGGESTED ANSWERS

- The reason not to include a photo with a CV is that employers might be instantly prejudiced against the way applicants look. This could be because they do not match the employer's stereotype of a competent person (see the interview with John Antonakis below), or because of prejudices against ethnic or religious groups, candidates of a certain age, etc. In some countries employers want to know personal details – age, marital status, whether the candidate has children, etc.; in other countries it is not normal to offer this information (although nothing stops interviewers asking about this in an interview).
- Ideally CVs should be totally honest, although most people probably exaggerate, or phrase things in an extremely positive way, where they think they can get away with it. It is *not* a good idea to tell lies that could be uncovered in an interview (such as 'I speak fluent Russian, Arabic, Chinese and Swahili').
- As discussed above, hobbies and interests can reveal candidates' skills and motivations.

- Although most people would presumably prefer *not* to work for someone who was prejudiced against their origin or religion, not everybody has the luxury of choosing their employer along these lines, especially in situations where employment is scarce.
- Targeting 30 different covering letters clearly takes time, but if untargeted letters are instantly rejected, it is time well spent.

Listening 1: Classifying the interviewee
▶ 1.9

John Antonakis, originally from South Africa, is Professor of Organizational Behaviour at the University of Lausanne. Shortly before the interview was recorded, he co-authored a remarkable article showing that people – both adults and young children – make almost instant judgements about other people's competence, based on their appearance. When shown photographs of rival candidates in past elections (in other countries, so the experimental subjects don't know the politicians in question), and asked which looks the more competent, the majority of people identify the winner. This implies that personal appearance is also likely to be a crucial factor in job interviews, as the interview with Antonakis will show.

See John Antonakis and Olaf Dalgas, 'Predicting Elections: Child's Play!', *Science* 27 February 2009, Vol. 323. no. 5918, p. 1183.

The interview with John Antonakis was not recorded by a professional sound recordist, and the quality is not as good as most of the other Listenings.

We have kept the original recording because it provides practice in authentic listening. Even the most articulate speakers hesitate, make false starts, repeat words, and so on. (These features of spoken language are generally not reproduced in the Audio scripts in the Student's and the Teacher's Books.) Listening to authentic speech is different from listening to actors reading transcripts of interviews.

AUDIO SCRIPT

JOHN ANTONAKIS There is a saying in English that 'One does not get a second chance to make a first impression.' This statement is very important because what it suggests is that when individuals judge a target individual, they make a decision about that target based on, on very small slithers of information. So it is very important that the person who is in an interview setting comes very well prepared, in terms of job knowledge, or knowledge about the post, or what background expertise and competences they have for the post, but also in their appearance, because every little slither of information, every little cue that the observer has on the target individual will influence how they categorize the target, and what is interesting is that research has shown that it only takes a few seconds for an interviewer to classify the target individual as being someone who is appropriate or not for a particular job.

Note

Antonakis seems to say *slither* rather than *sliver* (for a very small piece of information).

ANSWERS

1 The saying – 'One does not get a second chance to make a first impression' – means that the first impression you make on other people is important, because it remains in their mind, and it is hard to change it afterwards.
2 Interviewees should be very well prepared, know about the post they are applying for, know what background expertise and competences they have for the post, and also be careful about their appearance.
3 He cites research that has shown that interviewers judge or classify candidates or interviewees as suitable for a job or not in just a few seconds.

Listening 2: Confirming first impressions
▶ 1.10

AUDIO SCRIPT

JOHN ANTONAKIS Now the reason why observers make these rapid decisions about others in such situations is because they do not have full information on the target person. In a short interview that lasts half an hour or an hour, the interviewer cannot possibly know the target individual in terms of their personality, in terms of their intelligence. They're going to use small cues, and from these small cues they're going to make large inferences, so it's very important that the signals or the cues that the interviewee gives out are very concordant or close to what the interviewer expects. In psychology, we call this phenomenon 'confirmation bias'. So what happens is that the individual who's observing has some kind of stereotype or some kind of prototype in their heads about what a competent person should look like or what a good person for that particular post should look like. Now if you resemble that individual, they will try to confirm that initial impression by creating conditions in the interview that will make you succeed. If they don't like you, or if the initial impression is negative, the conditions that they will create in the interview will be such so that one fails. In other words, what we have observed in actual interview situations, or simulated situations where experimentally we, we have manipulated certain factors, is that interviewers don't change their minds very much from their initial impressions, so if someone is misclassified or classified badly in the beginning, it's very hard to recover that bad initial classification, again because of this confirmation bias, which is why it is so important to make a very good first impression.

ANSWERS

1A Yes: 'observers … do not have full information on the target person'
B No: 'the interviewer cannot possibly know the target individual in terms of their personality, in terms of their intelligence'
C Yes: 'They're going to use small cues, and from these small cues they're going to make large inferences'
D Yes: '… has some kind of stereotype or some kind of prototype in their heads about what a competent person should look like'
E No: they are biased as to what they think competent people are like. (Although interviewers probably consider themselves competent, they are interviewing people for posts that usually require different competences.)
F Yes: 'if you resemble that individual, they will try to … creat[e] conditions in the interview that will make you succeed. If they don't like you … the conditions that they will create in the interview will be such so that one fails'
G No, or not very much: 'interviewers don't change their minds very much from their initial impressions'
2 It means that interviewers are (unconsciously) biased towards individuals who resemble the stereotype or prototype they have in their heads about what a competent person or a good candidate for a job should look like.

Listening 3: Preparing for an interview
▶ 1.11

AUDIO SCRIPT

JOHN ANTONAKIS So in highly competitive situations where one really has to distinguish oneself, it's very very important in the interview situation to look natural, and by natural I mean that it doesn't seem like you are putting on an act. Of course it's a cat and mouse game in the interview setting so if one truly is natural one is natural because one is like that, or because one has practised to be like that. So again, the importance in preparation, I just cannot, one cannot underestimate. So, for example, if you've never had an interview before, it's very good to perhaps ask a peer, a friend, or someone who has more experience, or someone who already works, to give you a few practice runs, so that you can prepare yourself better, act in more natural ways, show a bit of, you know, positive body language, and confident body language, I mean small things like, you know, sitting up straight, smiling a little bit from time to time, maintaining good eye contact, using body gestures that are positive, those little things are like interest in the bank, they will add up, and they will really pay out in the long run. The reason why I say that is in the interview setting, the interviewer will probably pay as much, perhaps if not more attention, to things like appearance and non-verbal behaviour than actually what you say, so, you know, being natural and you know, sort of oozing positive body language and confident body language, I think is another important factor.

> **ANSWERS**
> - Look natural or act naturally (so it doesn't seem that you are putting on an act).
> - Practise before the interview with a friend with experience.
> - Use positive and confident body language and gestures (e.g. sit up straight).
> - Smile occasionally.
> - Maintain good eye contact.

Discussion: First impressions

There are no 'right answers' here. Many learners may deny that they judge people as quickly as Antonakis suggests they might, while also insisting that their first impressions are generally accurate; the same probably applies to many teachers!

It is conceivable that interviewers might become less biased simply by learning about what psychologists call confirmation bias, and the fact that they probably have stereotypes or prototypes in their heads.

Further tips for job interviews

There is no 'right answer' to the question. Some of these tips can be put to good use in the following Role play.

Role play: A job interview

There are three job advertisements at the back of the Student's Book on page 143, followed by a role card for the interviewer on page 144, but some preparation is needed before learners look at these.

The first task – studying the website of a large company – will presumably have to be done out of class, as homework. But first you or the class need to decide, probably in class, which company. It needs to be an organization that could conceivably have all three of the jobs advertised: Assistant Brand Manager, Assistant Supply Chain Manager, and Executive Assistant to the Chief Financial Officer. You could also substitute real jobs advertised by a local company, or a company to which the learners might apply in the future.

The second task, in which the learners choose one of the three positions on page 143 in the Student's Book and embellish their CV so that they are a potential candidate, can be done either in or out of class. In class, this could take 15–20 minutes. If this is done out of class, some of the learners can explain to the group in class which imaginary qualifications, skills and experiences they considered necessary, and why.

Anticipating (or for students with experience, discussing) the kind of questions asked at job interviews can be done in pairs or groups; how long this will take will depend on the experience and sophistication of the learners.

The role card for the interviewer is on page 144 in the Student's Book, and learners will need time to read through the notes and discuss them in pairs as part of their preparation. Once students have prepared their roles, the actual role play can be done twice, with different pairs, so that each learner gets a chance to interview and to be interviewed. Promising interviews can be repeated in front of the whole class.

6 Women in business

This unit contains extracts from an interview with Alison Maitland, co-author with Avivah Wittenberg-Cox of *Why Women Mean Business: Understanding the Emergence of our Next Economic Revolution* (Jossey-Bass, 2008); a newspaper article about legislation concerning women company directors; a discussion activity about male and female ways of thinking and behaving at work; and a role play about a company that wants to increase its number of women managers. The listening extracts put forward what appear to be very sound reasons for having more women directors and senior managers.

Lead-in

The answers to these questions will vary from country to country. However, very few business schools have more women than men teaching staff.

The essential reason for the relative absence of women managers is (presumably) the impact of childbearing and childcare on a woman's career.

Listening 1: Women in business – a strategic issue (1) ▶ 1.12

The two listening extracts are quite short and clear, but will probably need to be played twice. Learners can be asked to try to answer the general questions (and check them in pairs) after one listening, and the vocabulary questions after a second listening (again checking their answers in pairs).

AUDIO SCRIPT

ALISON MAITLAND   Well, there are several key reasons why women mean business, and why this issue is now really a strategic business issue – it's not a women's issue – and why it's time for CEOs to get serious about sex, as we say in the book.

One of these is the talent side of the equation, and that is that these days women actually account for the majority of university graduates. Six out of ten university graduates in North America, and in Europe, are women, so that's the talent pool, that's more than half of the world's, the developed world's, intellectual potential.

Another aspect is the market and the importance of women as consumers, and in the United States, eight out of ten consumer spending decisions are made by women these days, and that's not something peculiar to the US, it's a trend that's being followed by other countries, like Britain and France, Scandinavia, and we're going to see more of that. So women as earners earning money independently, spending, making big spending decisions, even in Japan two-thirds of car purchases are either made by or influenced by women.

> **ANSWERS**
>
> 1 Firstly, there are more women than men university graduates, so women make up over half of all the potential higher-level employees. Secondly, women themselves are important as consumers, and they also influence spending decisions made by men or couples.
>
> 2 All the potential qualified staff that a company could employ

Note

'It's time for CEOs to get serious about sex' is of course a jokey expression; *gender* would be a more usual word than *sex* in this context.

Listening 2: Women in business – a strategic issue (2) ▶ 1.13

AUDIO SCRIPT

ALISON MAITLAND   There's another reason which is very important in terms of profitability, and that is that now there are three big research studies that have shown a link between companies that have the most women in their senior management or on the board, and greater profitability. So those companies that have particularly a critical mass of women – that's to say about 30% plus of women on the board or in senior management – are

Unit 6 Women in business

Management

outperforming those that have no women or very few women in their senior teams, to the extent of, in one study there was an 83% higher return on equity amongst those companies that had the most women in their leadership ranks.

> **ANSWERS**
>
> Companies with a lot of women directors and senior managers are much more profitable than ones without.

Vocabulary

> **ANSWERS**
>
> 1 D 2 E 3 A 4 B 5 C

Discussion: The importance of women in business

If your learners are too young and poor ever to have made any major consumer spending decisions, you'll have to ask them to think about their parents, family, friends, etc.

The answer to the second question is presumably that women bring different ways of thinking to a business which, combined with more masculine ways of thinking, produce a large number of good ideas (about organization, procedures, products, services, marketing, etc.).

Reading: You're fired!

The text is extracted from an article in *The Guardian*, Thursday 6 March 2008.

Comprehension

> **ANSWERS**
>
> 1 40% of non-executive company directors must be female.
> 2 He says that there are very few experienced women working in the banking sector.
> 3 He says that they are 'apprentices' who need ten years' more experience before they can be competent company directors.
> 4 He says that companies will still get advice from people they have trusted for years, even though they are no longer on the board, so there will be parallel formal and informal systems.

Vocabulary

> **ANSWERS**
>
> 1 come across 2 compulsory 3 quota
> 4 voluntary 5 compliance 6 dissolution
> 7 apprentices 8 convert 9 accountability

Vocabulary note

Convert as a noun is stressed on the first syllable (*'convert*), unlike the verb *con'vert*, which is stressed on the second.

Discussion: Compulsory quotas

There are clearly no 'right answers' here.

Questionnaire: Ways of thinking

These statements are adapted from various chapters of *Why Women Mean Business*. Wittenberg-Cox and Maitland suggest that numbers 1, 3, 5, 7, 11, 13, 14, 15, 16 and 17 reflect mainly masculine ways of thinking. (They prefer 'masculine' to male, as there is also a minority of women who think this way.) They suggest that 2, 4, 6, 8, 9, 10, 12 and 18 are feminine ways of thinking. You can tell the learners this, if necessary, after they have completed and discussed their questionnaires. Some learners (and teachers) may vigorously resist 'essentializing' statements about 'how men/women think and act', but they cannot deny that such statements are widely made.

In-service learners will probably have more to say about these matters than full-time business students who have yet to work for any length of time. The former may have examples and anecdotes to offer.

Role play: Do we need more women managers?

There are five role cards at the back of the Student's Book on pages 145, 147, 149, 151 and 153. Depending on the number of learners, they can be asked to prepare a role individually, in pairs or in small groups. Select a good student for the CEO role, and emphasize the part of the role instructions that says 'Explain why you think this [the under-representation of women managers] is a problem', probably paraphrasing arguments from the **Listening** activities.

Director D is perhaps a delicate or 'politically incorrect' role, but you may have a learner whom this role fits.

Tell the learners that they should *not* simply read out their role card, but think about how they can express the beliefs outlined there in their own words. They should also think about possible responses to anyone who disagrees with them.

The (persuasive) arguments given to Directors A and B come from Wittenberg-Cox and Maitland's book. Which of these ideas the CEO in the role play will prefer may depend on the learner playing the role, or on the persuasiveness of the learners taking the other roles. The class can be invited to discuss the suggestions, and the meeting's (or the CEO's) conclusions, after the role play.

Writing

This memo or email could begin like this:

```
The CEO held a meeting with the non-executive directors to
discuss his belief that the company does not have enough women
managers and directors, and to see what can be done about this.

The following points were agreed ...
```

7 The different sectors of the economy

This is the first of four units on production. For a long time – certainly up to 2000, when the previous edition of this book was written – it was conventional to talk about the three sectors of the economy: agriculture, manufacturing and services. More recently, people have begun describing activities like ICT, consultancy, R&D, the news media, tertiary education, and so on, as belonging to a quaternary sector, which explains the revised title of this unit.

The unit includes a description of part of the economic infrastructure, seen from an aeroplane, extracted from David Lodge's *Nice Work*, which was published in 1989, before the notion of the quaternary sector became well known. There are also discussion activities and a reading about the pros and cons of manufacturing, as compared with service industries, and a listening involving business news items about different economic sectors.

Most governments encourage and welcome advanced service sector activities and companies, so the major discussion topic is the future of manufacturing in advanced countries. The emphasis on manufacturing explains why this unit has been moved to an expanded section on production.

Lead-in

The upper photo shows fields (primary sector) in the background, a quarry and cement works (primary and secondary sectors) on the right, a railway (tertiary sector) running diagonally across the picture, and housing and a football pitch in the foreground.

The lower photo shows the Millennium Dome at Greenwich in London, built for a temporary exhibition in 2000 and now a venue for concerts and sporting events. In front of the Dome is housing and various industrial units, with some wasteland and a cement works to the right. To the left of the Dome is a major road which leads to a tunnel under the River Thames, a gas storage tank, etc. Across the river on the left is Canary Wharf, with office buildings, bank headquarters, etc. With the help of Google Maps and Google Earth, and enough time to waste, you could probably identify every building!

Reading: Another cup of tea

The extract is from David Lodge's novel, *Nice Work* (London: Penguin, 1989), p. 269. Robyn, the university English lecturer, had never previously thought about economic matters before she met the managing director of a manufacturing company, so thinking about all this while looking out of the aeroplane (AmE: airplane) window is something of a revelation to her.

> **ANSWER**
>
> The text suggests that most people take for granted the amazing complexity of the economic infrastructure.

Vocabulary notes

It is probably not necessary for learners to understand every word in this text. But since they will ask … ! A *semi* is a semi-detached house, almost a symbol of suburban middle-class life in Britain. *Pebble-dashed* means that the bricks are covered with lots of small stones stuck in a thin layer of cement.

German speakers may confuse *warehouse* with *Warenhaus* (department store); French speakers may wrongly think *inhabit* is a negative word like the French *inhabité* (uninhabited).

A possible **additional exercise** related to this text would be to describe other processes, along the lines of Lodge's description of all the activities that precede boiling water in a kettle. For example, what has been done that enables you to pick up and use a pencil, brush your teeth, look in a mirror, and so on.

Comprehension

> **ANSWERS**
>
> 1 Tiny fields (the primary sector), factories (the secondary sector), and railways, motorways, shops, offices, and schools (the tertiary sector)
>
> 2 *Suggested answers*
>
> | primary sector | secondary sector | tertiary sector |
> | --- | --- | --- |
> | digging ore/bauxite
mining coal | assembling
building
cutting metal
laying cables
milling metal
pressing metal
smelting ore
welding metal | advertising products
calculating prices
distributing added value
maintenance*
marketing products
packaging products*
pumping oil*
transportation |
>
> * Some of these answers are open to discussion. For example, if maintenance involves cleaning office floors, this is a tertiary service, but if it involves replacing broken windows or overhauling machines, this is closer to building or construction, and should consequently be considered a secondary sector activity. Similarly, designing product packaging is a tertiary sector service, but the physical activity of packaging products can be considered part of the production process, which is a secondary sector activity. If pumping oil is understood as extracting oil by pumping water into bore holes, this is a primary sector activity, but if it is understood as pumping oil to or from a refinery, it is perhaps a tertiary sector transport activity.
>
> 3 Other primary sector activities include farming (agriculture), fishing and forestry. Other secondary sector activities include manufacturing, transforming and processing. Other tertiary sector activities include financing, designing and retailing.

The quaternary sector

This is quite hard to answer definitively. The advertising industry clearly uses a lot of computer applications; prices may be calculated using spreadsheets and other financial applications; packaging is almost certainly automated; assembly may be entirely automated, etc. Some of the other primary and secondary sector activities will use information technology; others will still largely involve manual labour.

Discussion: Your place in the economy

You might want to do some internet research to get statistics for the third question (or set it as a task for the learners). For the moment, statistics on the 'quaternary sector' are hard to come by.

Reading: Manufacturing and services

The seven statements here present arguments in support of having either services or manufacturing in advanced countries.

> **ANSWERS**
>
> Statements 1, 3, 4 and 7 are in support of manufacturing in advanced countries.
> (1 states that a lot of service sector jobs depend on manufacturing industry; 3 points out that all the world's major economies export a lot of manufactured goods; 4 points out that relying on services alone can be dangerous; and 7 points out that many service functions, unlike high-quality

manufacturing, can be delocalized to cheaper countries.)

Statements 2, 5 and 6 are in support of services. (2 argues that advanced countries have expertise in things like education, R&D, computing, consulting, etc., rather than low-cost manufacturing; 5 argues that manufacturing will be delocalized because of high labour costs; and 6 argues that major cities in advanced countries should specialize in arts and entertainment and tourism rather than manufacturing and industry.)

There's no saying which statements learners will agree with. Statement 1 is indisputably true. The first sentences in statements 2, 3, 4, 6 and 7 are all equally unarguable, but it is not certain that the next sentence necessarily follows. Some would argue with the 'inevitably' in statement 5. Statement 3 contains a sentence ('obviously') without any justification or reason.

Vocabulary

ANSWERS

1 exported goods   2 real estate (largely AmE)
3 labour   4 to delocalize   5 to outsource

Listening: The business news

Because there is a lot to listen for and write down here, it might be a good idea to have the learners work in threes. One can complete the first two columns, the second can complete the third and fourth columns, and the third can write down the figures in the last one. They can then compare and check and complete their answers. The learners will probably need to check their answers against the audio script too, perhaps while listening a final time.

NOTE

A trillion has 12 zeros: 1,000,000,000,000.

AUDIO SCRIPT

1 World oil prices have continued to fall today, with US sweet light crude dropping more than $3 to $63.20. Several members of OPEC, the 13-nation producers' group, which is responsible for producing about 40% of the world's total supply, want to cut output by at least one million barrels a day to increase prices.

2 US software giant Microsoft has posted profits and sales figures well above analysts' expectations. The company made a $4.37 billion profit during the first three months of its financial year, up from $4.29 billion a year ago, while turnover rose 9% to $15.06 billion.

3 In South Korea, Hyundai Motor Company has reported a 38% fall in third-quarter net profit, which was slightly better than expected, in a difficult year. Hyundai say that although global auto demand is shrinking, demand for smaller cars is rising. German car maker Daimler has reported a €213 million profit for the quarter, a dramatic turnaround from the €1.5 billion loss it made in the same period a year ago.

4 Although the service sector represents three-quarters of the British economy, a report published today by an American consulting company suggests that British manufacturers are still doing well. The UK is currently the world's sixth-largest manufacturer, but the country appears set to remain in the top ten for the next 15 years. Even though it is expected to slip to ninth place by then, its share of global manufacturing value added is forecast to dip by just one percentage point.

5 Mixed news from the airline sector today. While figures from the Association of European Airlines show that airline traffic has fallen for the first time in 25 years, because of the economic slowdown, Airbus has published its latest Global Market Forecast, which foresees a demand for some 24,300 new passenger and freight aircraft valued at US$ 2.8 trillion between now and 2026. This will create an average annual delivery of some 1,215 aircraft. The current decrease in traffic is expected to be temporary, and the long-term forecast for passenger traffic is that it is expected to grow at an average rate of 4.9% per year.

6 In another study published today, it is predicted that the rapidly growing biofuel market, involving cereals, sugar, oilseeds and vegetable oils, will keep farm commodity prices high over the next decade. The study, co-written by the Organization for Economic Cooperation and Development and the UN Food and Agriculture Organization, predicts prices will rise by between 20% and 50% in the next ten years.

Writing: The business news

This can be done in pairs. After writing their stories, the learners can read them out to the class or another pair. The six news stories in the Listening activity can serve as models.

ANSWERS

News item	Which industry or industries are mentioned?	Which economic sector or sectors are involved?	Which companies or organizations are named?	Is this good, bad or mixed news for the industry?	What figures are mentioned?
1	Oil	Primary	OPEC (Organization of the Petroleum Exporting Countries)	Bad	$3 fall to $63.20; 13 nations; 40% of supply; 1m barrels
2	Software	Secondary (production), tertiary (services) and quaternary (IT)	Microsoft	Good	$4.37bn profit; 3 months; $4.29bn; 9% rise in turnover to $15.06bn
3	Cars/automobiles	Secondary	Hyundai, Daimler	Good (or at least better than expected)	38% fall in profit; 3rd quarter; 213m profit; 1.5bn loss
4	Manufacturing	Secondary, tertiary and quaternary (the consulting company)	An American consulting company	Good	6th largest manufacturing country; top 10; 15 years; 9th place; 1% dip in global manufacturing value added
5	Airlines and aeroplane/airplane manufacturers	Tertiary and secondary	Association of European Airlines, Airbus	Mixed	25 years; 24,300 new aircraft; US$ 2.8 trillion; 1,215 planes a year; 2026; 4.9% annual passenger traffic growth
6	Farming/agriculture, biofuels	Primary and secondary	Organization for Economic Cooperation and Development (OECD), UN Food and Agriculture Organization (FAO)	Good	Price rises of between 20% and 50%; 10 years

8 Production

For a manufacturing company, production is obviously one of the four key functions, along with human resources, marketing and finance. This is the second of four units on production; the next two concentrate on supply chain logistics and quality.

This unit contains vocabulary and reading exercises relating to production capacity and inventory decisions; extracts from an interview with Alan Goodfellow of Leica Microsystems in Cambridge in which he talks about purchasing and low-cost manufacturing; an extract from Thomas Friedman's well-known book *The World Is Flat: A Brief History of the Twenty-first Century*, about what he calls (with tongue in cheek) 'The Dell Theory of Conflict Prevention'; and a case study about potential procurement risks for a multinational hi-tech manufacturer.

Lead-in

The **cartoon** might provide a good lead-in to the subject. Are your learners likely to go into manufacturing, or are they more interested in making money, probably in the financial industry, than in working in manufacturing industry?

- Production managers coordinate all the people and equipment involved in the manufacturing process, and try to ensure that production runs smoothly. Quality managers have to assure the quality of the products they make or the service they are responsible for, and also try to improve it.
- Production and operations managers should presumably be interested in making products or providing services. They usually need a lot of technical knowledge (about manufacturing processes) and mathematical abilities.
- The objectives of the production department are usually to produce a specific product, on schedule, at minimum cost. But there may be other criteria, such as concentrating on quality and product reliability; producing the maximum possible volume of output; fully utilizing the plant or the workforce; reducing lead time; generating the maximum return on assets; ensuring flexibility for product or volume changes, and so on. Some of these objectives are clearly incompatible, and most companies have to choose among price, quality and flexibility. There is an elementary trade-off between low cost and quality, and another between low cost and the flexibility to customize products or to deliver in a very short lead time.

Vocabulary: Industrial production

> **ANSWERS**
>
> 1 D 2 I 3 H 4 A 5 E 6 D 7 C 8 B 9 G

Vocabulary notes

The word *inventory* is used in both America and Britain. In Britain *stock* is sometimes used with the same meaning, although it also has a financial meaning (see British and American usage in **Unit 17**).

Location in English, meaning place, is of course not the same as *location* in French, meaning rental.

Reading: Capacity and inventory

> **SUGGESTED ANSWERS**
>
> 1 A and E 2 C 3 D 4 A and E 5 A 6 D 7 F
> 8 E 9 F 10 E 11 B 12 E 13 B 14 E
> 15 B and F

Notes

1. A long lead time means you can't start producing something quickly, but this isn't a problem if you have a sufficient inventory.
2. A large facility allows you to have a large production volume.
3. A large facility probably requires a lot of staff; it is sometimes easier to find staff if you have smaller factories in different locations. Logistics and material flow are clearly more complicated in larger facilities.
4. As with (1), this can be avoided by having a large inventory.

5 Lost sales and market share would arise from insufficient capacity (or insufficient inventory, which is not one of the six headings).
6 Labour relations tend to be worse in larger factories.
7 These are many of the disadvantages of having a large inventory in a single sentence!
8 These are among the advantages of having a large inventory.
9 These are further disadvantages of having a large inventory.
10 This is a basic reason to have an inventory.
11 If a factory is too large, some workers may not be needed if demand falls.
12 These are advantages of holding inventory from the supply point of view.
13 This could be another consequence of having excess capacity, or surplus workers.
14 This is a financial advantage of large production runs and inventories, although there are also financial disadvantages.
15 These could be two situations that would force companies to reduce prices.

Vocabulary note

Excess in heading B has a negative connotation (unlike *spare* capacity which could be an advantage).

Listening 1: Purchasing

AUDIO SCRIPT

ALAN GOODFELLOW Obviously one of the main goals of any company is to drive down the cost of raw materials and components that are used in manufacture, and Leica uses a number of techniques to achieve that. Firstly as part of the Danaher group they have the leverage of global buying power, that helps, that helps enormously because we can share suppliers with other companies within the Danaher group, and we also use techniques like, for example the reverse auction, which is a technique where we allow suppliers to bid for our business. It's rather like eBay in reverse in that they post on an internet site the lowest price with which they would do business with us and compete against each other in that way. Of course this has to be very carefully managed and there are a number of strategies in its use because price is not everything, we also have to guarantee quality, and we have to guarantee that the company can supply with reliability to that given price, so it's just one tool and even once the price has been determined we may not in fact choose the lowest price because we may deem another supplier to have an advantage with quality and delivery, but it's a useful tool used in that area.

ANSWERS

1 Driving down (reducing) the cost of raw materials and components
2 They have the leverage of global buying power, meaning that they can buy in large quantities for all their companies at once.
3 The company announces what materials and components it wants, and suppliers state the lowest price they are prepared to offer.
4 Because instead of prices rising, as in a standard auction, the buyer can choose the lowest offer
5 Other criteria, such as quality and reliability, are also important.
6 Leica may not in fact choose the lowest price.

Listening 2: Low-cost manufacturing

AUDIO SCRIPT

ALAN GOODFELLOW Well, the products are very high-tech, but Leica has always used low-cost region. I wouldn't describe it as outsourcing because they are factories owned by Leica. For example, we've had a factory in Singapore for 35 years and in China for 12 years which is a very long time in this industry, so they're wholly owned by Leica, not outsourced, but they provide low-cost manufacturing and we are able to maintain quality because they are wholly owned by Leica.

Yes, when we first set up the company in China there were a great many problems, mainly to do with training local staff, but particularly staff

42 Unit 8 Production

Production

retention, because the economy was booming so much, we found that after training staff, bringing them up to the standards we expected, they were very attractive to other companies and could easily move and take their skills elsewhere, so there was a constant process of training and retraining, it was very hard to retain staff.

> **ANSWERS**
>
> 1 They are countries that provide low-cost manufacturing.
> 2 Because the factories are owned by Leica
> 3 It was hard to keep or retain skilled staff because the economy was booming and they could easily move to another company.
> 4 1 training   2 staff retention   3 booming
>   4 skills   5 retraining   6 retain

Reading: 'The Dell Theory of Conflict Prevention'

The extract is from Thomas Friedman, *The World Is Flat: A Brief History of the Twenty-first Century, Release 3.0* (New York: Picador, 2007), pp. 587–8.

This is the first of two extracts from Friedman's well-known book, which is being updated in successive paperback editions (hence the '*Release 3.0*' in the title above). Thomas Friedman is an American writer and journalist, and a *New York Times* columnist; he is *not* to be confused with the Chicago school monetarist economist Milton Friedman.

As to how convincing Friedman's argument is, only time will tell whether 'No two countries will *ever* fight a war against each other as long as they are both part of the same global supply chain' is correct. It still holds true at the time of writing, though there could be other reasons for the lack of conflicts between these countries.

Comprehension

> **ANSWERS**
>
> 1 Because people in these countries work to provide goods and services for international companies, which increases their standards of living

> 2 Because it has been active in sourcing products from suppliers in many countries (in which there had previously been 'really disruptive events' such as conflicts between them)
> 3 They would probably lose their place in that supply chain for a long time.
> 4 It has brought prosperity and stability to a number of countries.

Vocabulary

> **ANSWERS**
>
> 1 embedded   2 standards of living   3 founder
> 4 risk premium   5 equity   6 disruptive
> 7 exponentially   8 procurement   9 prosperity
> 10 stability

Role play

This can either be an ad hoc meeting, or you can select someone to chair each group. The meeting doesn't need any preparation, as learners can be expected to know something about the three continents.

What the learners decide, especially about delivery times, will depend on where they (or their imagined assembly plant) are. At present, South America does not have a reputation for manufacturing hi-tech components, but if it did, they might well be low-cost. Some Asian countries have a reputation for being low cost, but not all of them (e.g. Japan). Low cost often correlates with low quality, but again, not in the case of Japan, South Korea and, increasingly, other Asian countries. Japan certainly has a reputation for reliability. Western Europe has a reputation for having higher costs than Asia. Some European countries have a particular reputation for quality and reliability (Switzerland, Germany, Sweden, etc.).

Writing

This email should have introductory and concluding sentences, and the body of the text could be arranged either by the five aspects of supply, or by the three geographical regions.

9 Logistics

This unit is largely about supply chains – the sequence of organizations and activities involved in acquiring components and raw materials, and producing and delivering goods or a service to the final consumers. Supply chaining has been greatly influenced by production processes, originating in Japan, that seek to minimize the quantity of inventory held by companies, and by advances in information technology. The unit contains a text about inventories, push and pull strategies, Just-In-Time (JIT) production, and so on; listening activities in which Alan Goodfellow of Leica Microsystems talks about inventory levels, Kanban and MRP; a second extract from Thomas Friedman's book *The World Is Flat*, about Wal-Mart's supply chain; and a short case study about potential supply risks in various industries.

Lead-in

The questions reprise the discussion about capacity and inventory in **Unit 8**. Satisfying current demand while holding the minimum of inventory is financially efficient, but does not allow organizations to meet an unexpected increase in demand. Holding a large inventory in case of increased demand allows a business to satisfy all potential customers, but comes at a cost – cash tied up in unsold goods.

Vocabulary: Pull and push strategies

Doing this exercise first may simplify the subsequent reading task.

> **ANSWERS**
>
> 1 D 2 C 3 A 4 B 5 G 6 E 7 F 8 H

Reading: Pull and push strategies

> **ANSWERS**
>
> 1 Manufacturing companies can produce …
> 2 With a pull strategy …
> 3 In other words, this is a …
> 4 This replenishment strategy was …
> 5 Historically, Kanban was …
> 6 Apart from JIT …
> 7 With a push strategy …
> 8 Supplies are scheduled …

Notes

The terms and abbreviations Just-In-Time, Kanban and MRP are used in many languages, as a quick Google search reveals.

What the text does not mention is that early push strategies were based on Materials Requirements Planning (MRP, later called MRP1). Most of these systems were later replaced by Manufacturing Resources Planning (MRP2), which combined MRP1 and capacity planning with a better control system.

Comprehension: Pull and push strategies

> **ANSWERS**
>
> 1 A 2 E 3 D 4 B 5 C

Listening 1: Inventory, Kanban and MRP ▶ 1.17

AUDIO SCRIPT

ALAN GOODFELLOW   Yes, nowadays companies do not want to hold inventory. Inventory is capital tied up that could otherwise be used to grow the business, so there are always pressures to keep inventory as low as possible. Now throughout the business of course we need inventory, we need equipment that we demonstrate to the customer, and we need certain stocks of materials used in manufacture, but always the strategy is to have the suppliers deliver when it's needed in the production process, and that can keep us agile, it enables us to react to sales and market demands without stocking large amounts of inventory which, as I said, has a large cost

Production

implication. So we move the responsibility to the suppliers to deliver to our factories when the demand is there.

The manufacturing processes in Leica tended to be based on MRP, which is Material Requirements Planning, quite a sophisticated IT-based forecasting of the parts needed for production, but under Danaher we've changed that to a Kanban system which is a pull system. When a part is used it's immediately replaced by another in that bin and it pulls all the way through to the manufacture, so it's not Just-In-Time as such, but it is a direct link between the demands of the customer on finished products and the supply of the components from our individual suppliers.

ANSWERS

1 Because it costs money, and uses ('ties up') capital that could be spent on developing ('growing') the business
2 To manufacture their products, and to demonstrate them to (potential) customers
3 They have their suppliers deliver materials to their factories when they are needed ('when the demand is there').
4 The company changed from an MRP system to a Kanban system.
5 Because there is a small inventory of each product

Listening 2: Leica's supply chain
▶ 1.18

AUDIO SCRIPT

ALAN GOODFELLOW As you can imagine for a global company of our size it's quite a complex supply chain. We have at the moment nineteen selling units selling in different countries around the world, and nine business units manufacturing the products that are sold, and often we need to consolidate products together to ship to the customer at one time, so the supply chain therefore becomes complicated. You'll have a business unit in one country, for example Singapore, that will manufacture parts themselves, most particularly the optics, which are the key parts of these systems, but also take sub-assemblies from suppliers, produce a unit which will then in some cases be shipped to Europe for consolidation with other parts before sending on to the end customer.

And then following all of this trail of course are the financial transactions and documents that allow you to invoice the customer in the local language of that customer and the local currency. The main goal is that the customer always deals with a local party in his own language, his own currency, and where he can get local service, and all of this supply chain is transparent to him. Big challenge for the company of course is delivering on time, when you're dealing with this global operation, and that's how we have to balance local stock which is always very expensive, we try and drive down inventory, we do not want inventory, but we have to balance the needs of local customers and the fast turnover of stock with the cost of keeping that inventory.

ANSWERS

1 The business units manufacture products and the selling units sell them.
2 No; sometimes it uses sub-assemblies from suppliers.
3 So that a customer's order is shipped (and delivered) all at the same time
4 Leica tries to make sure that customers always get local service, in their own language, and are quoted prices in their own currency.
5 It is easier to satisfy customers' needs and deliver products quickly if you have inventory stored near the customer, but the convenience of this must be balanced against the cost.

Reading: Supply-chaining

The text is from Thomas Friedman, *The World Is Flat: A Brief History of the Twenty-first Century, Release 3.0* (New York: Picador, 2007), pp. 151–2. (A previous extract from this book appears in **Unit 8**.)

This exercise can be done as an extensive reading; learners do not necessarily need to know every word (e.g. *perch, scores, sweeps, coastal, finale*, etc.).

> **ANSWERS**
>
> Friedman is clearly very impressed with Wal-Mart's distribution center (BrE: centre).

Comprehension

> **ANSWERS**
>
> 1 **a** bar codes **b** truck **c** merchandise
>   **d** conveyor belt **e** scans **f** signal
>   **g** supplier **h** delivered **i** stores **j** loaded
>
> **Note**
> These are the words in the text, but others are possible:
> **b** lorry **c** goods **h** sent **i** shops
>
> *Correct order:*
>   1 A Wal-Mart truck …
>   2 The goods are unloaded …
>   3 The boxes are placed …
>   4 The small conveyor belt …
>   5 A machine reads …
>   6 Electric arms guide …
>   7 This belt leads to …
>   8 The products are delivered …
>   9 A customer buys …
>   10 The cashier scans …
>
> 2 Friedman describes the automated system in the distribution centre as a 'show'.
>
>   He describes the conveyor belts as streams and rivers, because that's what they look like from above (from the 'viewing perch' in the distribution centre).
>
>   He describes the whole complex operation as a never-ending symphony in multiple movements, because symphonies consist of several movements and involve complex arrangements of a lot of 'components' or instruments and melodies, and this one has no finale.

Writing

This summary can take most of its words from Friedman's text, presumably missing out the metaphors.

> **MODEL ANSWER**
>
> Trucks deliver merchandise from suppliers at loading docks. At each loading dock boxes are placed on conveyor belts. These little conveyor belts lead to a bigger one. An electric eye reads the bar codes on each box as it travels along the belt. The large conveyor belt divides into smaller ones, and electric arms guide the boxes to Wal-Mart trucks, which deliver them to Wal-Mart stores across the country that have ordered these products.
>
> When a consumer buys a product in a store it is scanned, and a signal is sent to the product's supplier. The supplier receives the computerized signal and manufactures another item of that product, and ships it to Wal-Mart, and the cycle starts again.

Reading: Manufacturing supply chain work flow

> **ANSWERS**
>
> 1 The sales department identifies a need for a product, and tells the marketing department about it.
> 2 The marketing department researches the project, and forwards a detailed business plan to the Business Unit Manager.
> 3 The senior business managers make a decision on the project.
> 4 The plan is approved and passed to the analysts to prepare and implement the manufacturing process.
> 5 The analysts pass details of raw materials and components to purchasing.
> 6 The purchasing, logistics and transport departments plan the purchase of materials and their delivery to the manufacturing plant.
> 7 Suppliers receive orders and despatch raw materials and components to the manufacturing site on agreed dates.
> 8 The product is manufactured.

9. Finished goods are put into inventory in a warehouse awaiting orders, and the company computer system is updated.
10. Customers place orders through customer services.
11. Customer services take orders and input them to the computer system.
12. The order is sent to the warehouse.
13. The transport company collects the consignment and delivers it to the customer.
14. As stock has now been used, the computer system generates a request for new stock.
15. The re-order process generates a request to the purchasing department to place new orders with the suppliers.

Case study: Risk analysis

Companies try to minimize foreseeable risks, but there is always the danger of what the US Secretary of Defense Donald Rumsfeld once famously called 'unknown unknowns'.

> **SUGGESTED ANSWERS**
> - A British car factory sourcing components from Britain, Europe and Asia would face just about every risk possible: wars and conflicts in any of these areas; labour problems (strikes, etc.) at the producers or in the transport industry; damage to goods in transit; etc.
> - The fruit and vegetable department of a national supermarket chain would face potential temporary shortages in supply due to climatic or market conditions, and would probably have a wide network of local and not-so-local suppliers.
> - A tourist industry company hiring seasonal workers would probably always face competition from other employers, especially if it only wished to offer seasonal work to skilled employees; it would probably need to have potential alternative sources of supply.

Writing

This short report could be written individually or by pairs or small groups. It could have an introduction, stating its objectives or terms of reference (why it was written and who for), followed either by two sections, one listing the risks and the other the actions recommended, or a series of paragraphs each outlining one potential risk and a recommended course of action.

For example:

> This report was written by _____ at the request of _____ , to attempt to identify the potential supply chain risks for our _____ business. The major risks that we have identified are a) _____ , b) _____ and c) _____ .
>
> We suggest minimizing these risks as follows. Concerning a), we recommend _____ . Regarding b), we think that the company should _____ . In relation to c), we believe that we need to _____ .

10 Quality

This unit contains a discussion about quality, a text about TQM (Total Quality Management), listening exercises based on an interview with a manager responsible for setting up new hotels in Britain, and a role play about quality decisions in a hotel chain.

Lead-in

These questions should generate the vocabulary often used in relation to quality (*performance, appearance, reliability, durability*, and so on) and that related to poor quality (*repairs, replacing, complaints*, etc.).

> **SUGGESTED ANSWERS**
> - A small car is probably a relatively cheap one (luxury cars tend to be big). It will not perform like an expensive sports car, but it should be reliable and durable. It may not have as many features as larger cars, but should still have a good appearance.
> - A raincoat should keep you dry, i.e. be waterproof, and also last a reasonable length of time, and look good: appearance is probably important. 'Serviceability' might also be important: can you just put it in the washing machine, or does it have to be dry-cleaned?
> - A good laptop computer should probably be sturdy but light, come with a good quality screen, good quality sound, up-to-date software, a wi-fi card, a lot of memory, and so on. It should be durable, i.e. it should last a number of years without needing to be repaired, even though people tend not to use the same computer for many years because of rapid advances in technology.
> - A mobile phone or internet provider should provide non-stop service, without breaks because of technical problems. Mobile or cell phones should work almost everywhere, except perhaps on the top of a high mountain or in the middle of the ocean. And their prices should be competitive.
> - A good insurance company offers policies that are easy to understand, and deals with claims quickly and efficiently.

Reading and discussion

The text is from the inside flaps of the cover of the original hardcover edition of Philip B. Crosby's book *Quality Is Free* (McGraw-Hill, 1979).

> **ANSWERS**
> 1 1 C 2 D 3 E 4 A 5 G 6 F 7 B
> 2 Further examples of avoidable expenses relating to a lack of quality include:
> - handling complaints
> - identifying the causes of defects
> - redesigning a product or system
> - implementing corrective action
> - repairing or replacing defective products
> - training or retraining personnel
> - losing customers or their goodwill, etc.

Reading: Total Quality Management

Business learners may well know the expression Total Quality Management (and its abbreviation TQM). Without giving away the content of the reading passage, you could ask some preliminary discussion questions, such as: Is *total* quality really necessary? For example, would the learners throw away an advertising leaflet that had a single grammar or spelling error, because this gives a poor impression of the company? Are such details important?

There's a saying in English: 'If a job's worth doing, it's worth doing well'; how about reversing this – if something's really worth doing, surely it's also worth doing badly?!

Comprehension

> **ANSWERS**
> 1 TQM was developed in America, but first taken up by the Japanese.
> 2 TQM aims at (but doesn't guarantee) 'zero defect' production and no waste.
> 3 TQM never stops because products, services and processes are always capable of being improved.
> 4 TQM requires all a company's staff to be involved in the search for continuously improving quality.
> 5 TQM considers quality to be more important than maximizing output or reducing costs.

An **additional activity** would be to have the learners make a short **presentation** summarizing the main ideas behind TQM. They could first write these out as bullet points, and make a presentation based on those. For example:

- TQM (or just Quality Management), developed in the 1940s by W. Edwards Deming, was first taken up by the Japanese after World War II.
- It involves an attitude and a corporate culture dedicated to providing customers with products and services that satisfy their needs.
- Products should have zero defects, and services should be as close to perfect as possible.
- In other words, the company or organization should do the right things, and do them right, the first time and every time.
- But because products, services and processes change, everything is capable of being improved all the time.
- TQM requires the staff in all a business's activities to be involved in the search for continuously improving quality.
- The entire staff should use their knowledge and experience to identify and correct faulty systems and processes.
- Production workers should be empowered to stop production to solve quality problems.

Discussion: Good and bad quality

If learners can think of organizations whose product or service quality could *easily* be improved, there are presumably evident reasons why the organization is not offering higher quality, probably related to cost, or a perceived price–quality ratio. Or perhaps because they have a dominant market position and can get away with poor quality.

Notwithstanding the exercise above about quality being free, and a lack of quality costing money, it is unlikely that significant quality improvements could be made to most products or services without a corresponding increase in costs and prices.

Discussion: A four-star hotel

A four-star hotel should probably have large, relatively soundproof rooms with comfortable furniture, a bath and shower, and probably amenities such as air-conditioning, a minibar, a safe, cable TV, internet access, etc. There will also generally be a restaurant, room service, multilingual reception staff, and private car parking. (You might also walk into your room the first time and find several lights on and the air-conditioning at full blast, and a welcoming message with your name on it on the TV screen. And, of course, the end of the toilet roll pointlessly folded into a triangle!)

Listening 1: Hotel customers and quality ▶1.19

Denis Frucot is French and, understandably, has a French accent. He also uses a few expressions and constructions that most native speakers would not use, but there seems no point dwelling on these.

> **AUDIO SCRIPT**
>
> **DENIS FRUCOT** If your guests have been satisfied with what they had and they think that the service you've offered is of quality they'll come back. If you are no quality or very little quality to the customers' perception they won't come back, it's as simple as that, so the more you can offer, the better the service you can offer, the more comprehensive it can be, the more, the more you'll be successful and the more you'll have a customer base, it's as, pretty much that.

After that, especially with what we do, the notion of quality is very subjective, it tends to come with the customers' perception of it.

For instance, a bed and breakfast, you have a pre-conceived idea of what the service is going to be like, your notion of quality will be, will revolve round the fact that they exceed these expectation[s] or they went below. If you find out that you have an en suite bathroom in a bed and breakfast and you've got some form of turndown service you'll be 'I'm coming back tomorrow, I'm staying a week!' Same opposite, if you find a dead cockroach in the middle of your bathroom, well certainly you have second thoughts about even spending one night, so it's pretty much like that.

ANSWERS

1 The fact that if customers are satisfied (they perceive the quality to be good) they'll come back, and if they are not, they won't
2 An en suite bathroom and someone who turns down your blankets or duvet, and a dead cockroach in the middle of the bathroom

Listening 2: Customer care ▶ 1.20

AUDIO SCRIPT

DENIS FRUCOT   Obviously, we're not a five-star hotel – Hotel du Vin as a group has always looked for, we aim at about three, four, but if we were to look and behave as a star rating system, but for that quality, for that level of conception, we tend to give a lot more. The service provided is usually of a higher standard. The service we offer, the notions we offer, revolves around the actual service that we provide. In order to give people the idea and that notion of quality which is very, as I said, very subjective, we have to emphasis[e] the customer care, we define what we call a guest's journey which revolves around, from the first impression they get from seeing it on a website to the last impression they get when they walk out the door of the hotel. You have to have friendly reception staff that know about the area, that know about Cambridge as if they were born there, although they are not, clearly, but they have to be able to get you a taxi whenever you need one, hairdressers, restaurants, it goes through a vast amount, array of things that people will not necessarily expect you to have but will be very, very impressed if you do, and really we try to embed that into absolutely every single member[s] of staff.

ANSWERS

1 He says that it is of a higher standard than the number of stars the hotels have would suggest, as they put a lot of emphasis on customer care
2 Friendly, knowledgeable and helpful reception staff

Listening 3: Selecting and training staff
▶ 1.21

AUDIO SCRIPT

DENIS FRUCOT   We have a very strong programme of progression for each member[s] of staff. All of my heads of department have come with me from a different hotel – I've opened four so far, I tend to hop around the country and I do that – but I've got a nucleon of people that I will, whenever I open a new one elsewhere I will call them or I'll go round the whole group and just select people that already have the philosophy of what we're trying to achieve, and then after that from the top down they train a smaller amount of people, reception for instance, all the girls in reception I was very adamant that I wanted local people, people that know Cambridge, because after that we have, I have at least two people, two persons in reception – head receptionist and her assistant, are both from within the company, so they know the brand – after that I take four people that know Cambridge very well, you've got at least a base to work on and they can exchange, it's interactive for both of them, as well with the idea of evolution within the company, whether it's here, whether it's elsewhere, but we open at a rate of about three hotel[s] a year at the moment so it's a lot of growing opportunity.

Production

> **ANSWERS**
> 1 He selects heads of department who have already worked in other hotels in the group, or people with the 'philosophy' of quality that he's looking for, who will train the other staff.
> 2 People from within the company, who know the brand, and local people who know the town very well, and so can give advice and information to customers

Role play: A hotel chain in trouble

There are four role cards at the back of the Student's Book on pages 145, 147, 149 and 152. The learners can prepare their roles in pairs or small groups. They can be asked to decide what they will say in the meeting, and how they will counter opposing arguments.

As always, it is important to select a learner to chair the meeting who is likely to be able to do it well. Quite how the role play will go is hard to predict. The Financial Director's cost-cutting suggestions are rather lame, and unlikely to find favour; his/her suggestion of selling or converting unprofitable hotels probably makes more sense. The Marketing Manager's suggestion of going downmarket would definitely be a lot cheaper than the Operations Manager's suggestion of going upmarket, and closing hotels for several months to rebuild them. But a persuasive learner could sway the others.

Writing

A press release announcing that the hotels were to be re-branded as low-cost hostels, or converted into luxurious four-star hotels, would be resolutely positive. An internal email explaining that costs were going to be reduced and prices increased would simply have to be factual.

> See also the role play 'Quality and personnel' in *Business Roles* by John Crowther-Alwyn (Cambridge University Press).

11 Products

This is the first of three units on marketing. It contains a text about products and branding strategies, an interview with the director of a chain of juice bars in Switzerland, and a case study about launching a business.

Lead-in

People's brand loyalties are unpredictable, but often include brands of clothing, food, cosmetics, personal hygiene products, alcoholic drinks, cigarettes, sports teams, newspapers and magazines, etc.

The reasons for brand loyalty can vary. Consumers may be satisfied with the quality and price of the brand, and so have no reason to change; they may consider a brand to be fashionable, and therefore desirable; they may be influenced by continuous advertising; or they may simply have unwittingly acquired a habit, which saves them the time and effort necessary to make a choice when they go shopping

Products that many people buy without even noticing the brand name might include stationery (ball-point pens, pencils, erasers, pencil sharpeners, note paper, writing paper, envelopes, and so on), as well as matches, salt, sugar, flour and other cooking ingredients.

Reading: Products and brands

Business learners – and even thoughtful consumers – may already understand the logic of branding. There is a lot of information in the text, but the concepts and vocabulary are all tested in the exercises which follow.

> ANSWERS
> 1 Products, product lines and product mixes
> 2 Branding
> 3 Branding strategies
> 4 Brand value

Comprehension

> SUGGESTED ANSWERS
> 1 Because both customers' needs and the market change, and because the company's products are at different stages of their life cycles, including some in the decline stage
> 2 In order to distinguish them from competitors' products
> 3 Corporate branding means including the company's name in all its products, while individual branding means giving each product its own brand name.
> 4 Because this allows them to occupy more space on supermarket shelves, and in this way get more sales and a bigger market share
> 5 Because of the value of their brands, and the future sales these brands will bring

Vocabulary

> ANSWERS
> 1 outlets 2 product mix 3 retailers 4 logo
> 5 packaging 6 brand recognition 7 shelves
> 8 market share 9 brand-switchers

Vocabulary note

The singular of *shelves* is *shelf,* and marketers often talk of occupying 'shelf space'.

Discussion: Brands and attitudes

There are, of course, no 'right answers' here.

An **additional activity** would be for learners to look at the current Top 100 brands on Interbrand's website at http://www.interbrand.com. Ask:

- How many of the brands do you recognize?
- For how many of these companies are you a potential customer?
- Why do you think you know these brands – from seeing their products, from advertising, from newspaper articles, etc.?

Alternatively, you could show the learners these companies' logos – or even just a small part of each logo – and see how many are instantly recognized.

Most of the companies and brands named in the text are widely known in developed countries (Nike, Starbucks, Apple Computer, The Body Shop, Philips, Virgin, Yamaha, Pampers, Pringles, Duracell, Gillette, Coca-Cola). Because of their individual branding strategy, Procter & Gamble will be less known to people who don't read the business pages in newspapers or the small print on products.

The top ten brands (at the time of writing), according to Interbrand, are:

1 Coca-Cola **2** IBM **3** Microsoft **4** GE (General Electric) **5** Nokia **6** Toyota **7** Intel **8** McDonald's **9** Disney **10** Google

An **additional question**: which of these brands are *not* American?
Answer: Nokia (Finland), Toyota (Japan)

Most of Interbrand's top 100 are international consumer-goods companies, but there are also a lot of financial institutions. The make-up of the top 100 can and does change; in autumn 2008, several large banks and insurance companies either went bankrupt or got taken over or had to be rescued by their governments.

Listening 1: Not just a juice bar
▶ 1.22

At the time of writing, Zeste4Life have three juice bars in the French-speaking part of Switzerland, and they plan to open several more. The interview with Melissa Glass was not recorded by a professional sound recordist, and the quality is not as good as most of the other Listenings. As her accent reveals, Melissa Glass is Australian.

AUDIO SCRIPT

MELISSA GLASS We launched a bar called Zeste Juice Bars. We sell a product that is a smoothie. We have two lines of products, we have smoothie which is a mixture of juice with frozen fruits, with either sorbet or yoghurt and ice, that's quite a thick drink, and the other thing we sell is freshly squeezed juice which is carrots juice, apple juice, there's orange juices and mixers of that to make different cocktails. We have a small side product of food as well, to complement the juice, so that people who come at lunchtime, they don't have to go to two places, they can buy something at ours and eat and drink at the same place, but in general our whole concept is based around a slogan of 'Zeste4Life', so it's about the image that we create, the whole, the energy behind it, the youth, the colours, the package, essentially. We're not, we don't consider ourselves just a juice bar.

ANSWERS

1 Smoothies – a mixture of juice with frozen fruits; freshly squeezed fruit juices; and a small side product of food
2 Because they are also selling a concept and an image of energy and youth; and they are selling food

Listening 2: The origin of smoothies
▶ 1.23

AUDIO SCRIPT

MELISSA GLASS OK, so the concept came, originally started in California, and that was about 20 years ago, at which point the concept was based just around juice. It progressed to be more based around smoothies. That concept then was taken to Australia in '99. I saw the concept in Australia grow in '99 through to 2001, where it became very popular, and you eventually saw bars like this all over the place. My husband and I decided that, we thought it was a product, a line of product or a concept that really wasn't existent in Switzerland, and we thought that it was a population, the Swiss are a population that would consume that sort of product and that there was a niche in the market. So we decided that we would launch Zeste Juice Bars, and we did that in 2004.

> **ANSWERS**
>
> 1 In California, with bars first selling fruit juices, and later smoothies
> 2 In Australia
> 3 Because the product didn't exist there and they thought the Swiss would buy it

Listening 3: Launching the product
▶ 1.24

AUDIO SCRIPT

MELISSA GLASS Launching a new product from scratch is quite difficult. First off we had to … we had the idea, we had to then do market research here obviously to work out, if the product would be, would be accepted and consumed here.

We had to do research into pricing, we had to do research into colours, what locations where it was going to be the most successful. We knew that obviously we needed high-frequency passage. The problem with that in Switzerland is the locations, the places with high passage are extremely expensive, so it's always a balance between getting somewhere that's got enough passage but not too, too expensive, because when you're selling a product that has a cost price of five francs you have to sell a lot of juices and smoothies to cover the base, the base cost. Apart from that we had to do obviously questionnaire friends, take surveys, we had to do, we also did trialling, sampling, we did a couple of parties at our place to try the different products, and to choose the different smoothies that we were going to start with.

We then had to come up with names as well, we had the big difficulty of deciding which language we were going to do it in, and we decided to take English for our names because that sort of followed where the concept came from, the base of the product, the origin, the origin of the product, and then we, we decided to launch in Lausanne because that was our home town. We knew the town very well, we knew the passage, we knew the frequence, we knew basically where the town works, the heart of the town, and we needed to test the product first off and then do our adaptations from that, and then launch in bigger towns like Geneva or Zurich or places like that, but it's important, it was important we decided to trial one store. We decided that one store, we would trial for one year and then after that we would consider expanding.

> **ANSWERS**
>
> 1 1 pricing 2 locations 3 high frequency 4 base cost 5 trialling 6 sampling
> 2 A lot of people (potential customers) walking past the store
> 3 Because the product originated in an English-speaking country (and is perhaps associated in customers' minds with warm climates like California and Australia)
> 4 To test or trial the product in one store for a year, and make any necessary adaptations, and then launch in bigger towns

Vocabulary note

Market research is used in British and Australian English; *marketing research* is more common in American English.

Case study: Researching a product concept

This case study can be done as rigorously as time permits. If there is time, the groups of learners could be asked to prepare their product concept out of class, and then present it to the class. They will need to present their product concept – what the business would offer, and where, and its name – and to explain how it would differ from existing businesses (if any). They could be asked to investigate commercial rents in their town, from property agencies' advertisements, or from official statistics provided by the local government. Learners studying marketing may know about pricing strategies.

If there is even more time, the learners could do the market research, either preparing a questionnaire and interviewing real people (in whatever language), or using the rest of the class as a focus group (which could of course substitute for presenting the product concept to the class), or doing the less exciting statistical research.

Marketing

- For a juice bar, you (the teacher) would want to know about products and prices, and how they would differ from any local competitors.
- For a taxi company, you would want to know where the taxis would be situated, and how customers would find them (in the street, by telephone, via the Internet, etc.).
- A home-delivery pizza service (as opposed to a restaurant) does *not* need expensive premises on a shopping street. It does require effective advertising, but this is the subject of a later unit.
- A gym and fitness centre needs expensive equipment, and location (perhaps with 'high-frequency passage') is important. You would definitely want to know how it would differ from any local competitors.
- For a language school, you would want to know which languages would be offered, who the potential customers would be, how the business would recruit teachers, etc.

A final question to the learners could be: If the research shows that there is not much interest in the product, would you abandon the idea, or launch the business anyway, trusting that the research was wrong, or that you could improve and adapt the service as you went along? (The right answer is, of course: abandon the idea.)

Writing

This could be done individually or in pairs or groups. The report could be as long and detailed as time permits.

12 Marketing

After the usual opening discussion questions and a vocabulary exercise, this unit contains a reading exercise about product life cycles, discussion activities about pricing and distribution channels, a text extracted from a well-known article in the *Harvard Business Review*, further listening exercises concerning the business talked about in **Unit 11**, and a case study about promotions.

Lead-in

There is no 'right answer' here. The first definition is succinct, and is often used to distinguish between the 'selling concept', which is presumed to be out-of-date and inefficient, and the 'marketing concept', which is assumed to be current and effective.

The second definition comes from *Marketing: Principles and Practices* by Dennis Adcock et al, first published in 1995. The most recent edition keeps the words in bold, but puts it in the past tense: 'marketing covers a wide range of activities, in fact everything related to what was once described as providing **the right product, in the right place, at the right price, and at the right time**' (4th edition, *Financial Times* / Pearson Education, *Financial Times* / Prentice Hall, 2001, p.1). The term 'marketing mix', to which this definition relates, was first used by Harvard professor Neil Borden in the 1950s to describe all the actions a company can perform in order to influence the consumer decision to purchase goods or services. In the early 1960s, E. Jerome McCarthy, another Harvard professor, suggested that the marketing mix consisted of the four Ps (see his *Basic Marketing: A Managerial Approach*, and all marketing textbooks since).

The third definition is similar to many others of the past decades, while the fourth one is a bit more modern, and rather more extreme, as it suggests that marketing doesn't so much involve identifying needs as anticipating and creating them.

(An **additional question**: can you give some examples of products you use that you didn't know you wanted until someone produced them? Older teachers may remember life before personal stereos, personal computers, the Internet, Google, eBay, Facebook, mobile phones, etc.; younger learners won't!)

Vocabulary: Basic marketing terms

> **ANSWERS**
>
> **1** distribution channel **2** wholesaler **3** market segmentation **4** product differentiation **5** market opportunities **6** market skimming **7** sales representative (often abbreviated to 'sales rep' or just 'rep') **8** product features **9** price elasticity **10** market penetration

Reading: The product life cycle

Learners should be able to work out most of the answers from the shape of the graph, the logic of competition, pricing, etc. Like a crossword, this exercise should get easier as it progresses.

> **ANSWERS**
> - Sales: 2 A 3 B 4 C 1 D
> - Costs: 1 E 3 F 2 G 4 H
> - Prices: 4 I 1 J 2 K 3 L
> - Promotion: 3 M 2 N 4 O 1 P
>
> Alternatively:
> - Introduction stage: D E J P
> - Growth stage: A G K N
> - Maturity stage: B F L M
> - Decline stage: C H I O

An **additional writing** exercise would be for the learners to combine the sentences into a four-paragraph text, adding phrases such as 'During the introduction stage', and perhaps combining sentences with connectors, e.g. 'During the maturity stage, sales volume peaks but the product's features may have to be changed because …'

Marketing

Discussion: Pricing

> **NOTES AND ANSWERS**
>
> 1 As mentioned in the vocabulary exercise and the exercise on product life cycles, companies with a new high-tech or high-quality product can use a price-skimming strategy to make maximum revenue before competing products appear on the market. Any company with anything approaching a monopoly can also charge high prices (look, for example, at many established European airlines). As mentioned in the previous exercises, companies with new products can also charge a low price (a market penetration strategy) in order to get a large market share before competitors appear on the market.
>
> 2 Books, for academic work or for leisure reading, may well fall into this category: they are often also available in libraries, so it is not essential to buy them. There are many other products that people buy more of if or when the price is reduced – CDs, computer games, clothes, etc.
>
> 3 Food of some kind is usually necessary, whatever its price. There are also high-quality goods for which producers can charge *very* high prices, as there are a sufficient number of consumers who think possessing the product gives them high status. This is called premium pricing or prestige pricing.
>
> 4 I'm convinced that I instantly round prices up in my head. But I'm also convinced I'm never persuaded against my better judgement by advertising, so I'm probably wrong on both counts.
>
> 5 It's usually established market leaders with large amounts of cash that win price wars, and competitors with smaller market shares that lose them. A personal recollection: in the summer of 1980, all the major US airlines cut their domestic ticket prices. You could fly coast-to-coast (e.g. New York to Los Angeles, or Boston to San Francisco) for a mere $120. So I gratefully did. Within two years, two of the airlines had gone bankrupt, and the remaining companies raised their prices dramatically, so the customers' gain was short-lived. Price wars are not to be confused with loss-leader pricing – deliberately selling some items at a price that doesn't make a profit. Supermarkets generally have a few of these, which attract customers who also buy other items with higher profit margins.

Discussion: Distribution channels

> **SUGGESTED ANSWERS**
>
> Producer – wholesaler – retailer – consumer is the traditional channel for many, if not most, consumer goods. This means that neither the producer nor the retailer needs a large warehouse. For exported goods, many companies work with agents. Producers often use their own sales staff for technical products sold to other companies (B2B): the sales reps are able to demonstrate and explain the products. Many publishers now sell books online, cutting out the retailer, and museum shops and football clubs send out a lot of mail-order merchandising catalogues. Customers can usually order goods by telephone as well as by mail or online. Telephone sales are also common for banking and insurance products (or what used to be called services).

Writing

> **MODEL ANSWER**
>
> Publishers often sell books to wholesalers who stock them in warehouses, and deliver small quantities to retailers (booksellers). Increasingly, however, people are ordering books online, which are delivered by mail.
>
> Producers of machines and technical equipment often have their own sales representatives, who visit potential customers. If they are selling machines abroad, companies sometimes work with local agents in each market.

Reading: Marketing is everything

These are short extracts from an often-cited ten-page article by Regis McKenna in the *Harvard Business Review*, January–February 1991. It begins with the classic example of the sales-driven company and the mass-produced product, the Model T Ford, and Henry Ford's famous line from his autobiography (*My Life and Work*, 1922).

As an example of the 'tell us what color you want' school of marketing McKenna gives the National Industrial Bicycle Company of Kokuba, Japan, which at the time offered made-to-order bicycles with no fewer than 11,231,862 variations!

McKenna's account of integrating the customer into the design of the product has perhaps been superseded by the 'wikinomics' principle discussed in **Unit 3**, which sometimes invites the whole world to integrate the company.

> **SUGGESTED ANSWERS**
>
> 1 They tried to change customers' minds and make them like the products they produced.
> 2 Because there was more competition, and because technology developed and allowed companies to change products to match what customers asked for
> 3 Market-driven companies work with customers to understand their strategies, and adapt their products to fit them, and in this way try to create a new market.
> 4 The old approach is all about testing and marketing a company's idea, rather than responding to a demand that comes from customers.
> 5 Because the main demand on companies first changed from controlling costs to competing with other companies with similar products, and then to serving customers
> 6 Fooling the customer and falsifying the company's image
> 7 Market-driven companies integrate the customer into the design of the product.
> 8 If you focus on your R&D you forget about the customer, the market and the competition.
> 9 Trying to increase your market share is like fighting over crumbs rather than trying to own the whole pie (or the whole market).
> 10 The real job or goal of marketing is to produce what customers need so well that you control (or own, or lead) the entire market for your products.

Note

There is a Calvin and Hobbes cartoon, reproduced in Chapter 1 of Steven Pinker's *The Stuff of Thought* (London: Penguin, 2008), in which Calvin takes a physics exam. Faced with the instruction 'Explain Newton's first Law of Motion in your own words', he writes 'Yakka foob mog. Grug pubbawup zink wattoom gazork. Chumble spuzz.' This is *not* what 'in your own words' means in question 10!

Listening 1: Promoting a juice bar
▶ 1.25

AUDIO SCRIPT

MELISSA GLASS After the launching of Zeste in Lausanne, in the beginning, as I said, it was quite difficult, we looked at different ways of attracting customers, we looked into different forms of marketing. The first, the first tactic on Lausanne was just sampling, we did sampling on the street, we, I sent out one of my staff members with little sample goblets, and people, little cups, and people then got to try our product, and I knew that if they tried our product they'd be happy – our product sells itself as far as taste. That was quite successful, but at the time we launched in October, so we were going into winter, again as I said before, the foot traffic was less, so then we decided what we were going to do was some sort of advertising campaign, something visual to get, to touch the people that, that hopefully they would come. This unfortunately was a very expensive experience. We went through a design agency, we designed posters to go into the buses, because the bus actually passed directly in front of our store. We saw the people in the bus, they didn't know who we were, what we did, and we, I felt we needed to touch these people. So we did a two-week campaign, which was rather expensive, to pay the time in the bus, also the production of the design of the, the flyer, and also the printing of the flyers. We went with the concept of having a fit woman with boxing gloves, with the theme of 'Get a, get a kick out of your vitamins and come to Zeste.' Unfortunately, what we realized wasn't on the pamphlet was enough information about the product, because the Swiss didn't know at that stage what a smoothie was. For them, this word didn't exist, so it wasn't a very effective campaign.

Note

The photo shows advertising pamphlets on a Swiss bus. Pamphlets, flyers or leaflets are placed in a narrow box. The pamphlet in the photo is *not* for Zeste Juice Bars, but a campaign for sponsoring young Swiss sports prodigies. (Notice the language used in the title.)

Marketing

ANSWERS

1 Sampling – giving away free samples of the products in the street
2 Because they are very confident about their product (which 'sells itself as far as taste' is concerned), so given a free sample, people would 'be happy', and perhaps become customers
3 The concept was emphasizing health and fitness and vitamins, but they found that the message was too indirect, without enough information about what smoothies are, which customers at the time didn't know.

Listening 2: The most effective form of promotion ▶ 1.26

AUDIO SCRIPT

MELISSA GLASS The most effective thing we've found is publicity in the papers, and in general free publicity, so my partner spends a lot of time contacting the journals, papers like the, the free ones in the morning, and trying to get free articles when we have a new product or something hip, or something changes. They're often keen to have new things, or new bits of information. That then hits the target straight away that day and people tend to take … the effect is immediate. Those articles don't have an effect a week later in general, but it has the effect that day or the next day and the idea is behind this for us is that we then convince that person by the product and the taste of the product, and that they will come back because of that.

ANSWERS

1 Free publicity – articles in newspapers
2 It has an immediate effect, but if new customers are convinced by the product, they will return, which can produce a permanent increase in sales.
3 Probably because articles based on press releases look like objective news, so people trust and believe them more than paid advertising

Case study: Promoting a new product

If the learners have recently thought about a product or service in **Unit 11**, they may want to use the same product or service here. Of course, their research results may *not* have been encouraging, in which case they should abandon their idea. But human nature being what it is, or business learners being what they are (optimistic, and not wanting to have spent time for nothing), few people want to interpret market research data negatively and give up on a product concept. This gives rise to an additional question: How many new products fail? Different marketing books give different figures, but it is usually said that over 80% of new products never become commercial successes. The figure must be even higher for new product concepts, as some are abandoned during the market research or test marketing phases, and never achieve a full commercial launch.

The learners have (presumably) yet to do **Unit 13** on advertising, but they will have some notions about this. A taxi company and pizza-delivery business would probably require a lot of advertising. Publicity is described in the second listening activity, and sampling in the first. Other sales promotions could include temporary price reductions or temporary free admission for the fitness centre and perhaps the language school.

Once the learners have established their promotion strategy they can present it to the class, and explain why they chose it, and see whether the class agrees that it is a good strategy.

Depending on time, learners can be asked to provide a more or less detailed promotional strategy. After presenting it to the class, they could also set it out in a memo or an email as a **Writing** activity.

See also the role plays 'Changing names' and 'New products' in *Business Roles* by John Crowther-Alwyn (Cambridge University Press).

13 Advertising

All language learners have some experience of advertising, as consumers or potential consumers, and should have something to say about this subject. This unit contains a text on advertising and viral marketing, discussion activities about different advertising and sales promotions techniques, a listening exercise based on authentic radio commercials, and an activity involving the preparation of a radio commercial.

Lead-in

There are few 'right answers' here, but here are some remarks.

Advertising professionals are confident that *everyone* is susceptible to advertising, including those who think they are far too rational and worldly-wise to be influenced by it.

It is often claimed that people living in and moving about cities, reading newspapers and using electronic media are potentially exposed to 3,000 advertising messages a day (e.g. in the article extracted in Unit 12, 'Marketing is everything' by Regis McKenna).

Advertising people talk about frequency or 'OTS' (opportunities to see) and the threshold effect – the point at which advertising becomes effective – but there is no reliable answer as to how many times a consumer needs to see a message: it depends on the product, the customer's interest, and the effectiveness of the advertising.

A famous (or perhaps infamous) article in the *Harvard Business Review* ('Businessmen Look Hard at Advertising', by Stephen A. Greyser and Bonnie B. Reece, May–June 1971), reported on a survey of top or senior managers subscribing to the journal. 85% of the respondents believed that advertising often persuades people to buy things they don't *need*, and 51% that it often persuades people to buy things they don't *want*. Your learners may well deny that this has happened to them.

Reading: Advertising and viral marketing

> **ANSWERS**
>
> 1 B   How companies advertise
> 2 A   Advertising spending and sales
> 3 D   Potential drawbacks of advertising
> 4 C   Word-of-mouth advertising and viral marketing

Comprehension

> **ANSWERS**
>
> 1 To inform (consumers about products and services), and to persuade (them to buy them)
> 2 To create advertisements and develop a media plan
> 3 Spending a fixed percentage of current sales revenue, spending as much as competitors, and increasing current spending in order to increase sales
> 4 It is expensive, it doesn't always reach the target customers, and it isn't always welcome as it interrupts people when they are trying to do something else.
> 5 Blogs, online forums, commenting on blogs and social networking sites, podcasts, viral videos

Vocabulary

> **ANSWERS**
>
> 1 advertising agencies   2 advertising campaign
> 3 brief   4 target customers   5 (advertising) budget   6 media plan   7 comparative–parity method   8 (free) sample   9 word-of-mouth advertising   10 viral marketing

Vocabulary note

In Britain, *media* is plural, so, for example, television is *a medium*. In the US, *media* is often also used as a singular.

Writing

> **MODEL ANSWER**
>
> Traditional advertising is expensive and doesn't always reach the target audience. If it does reach the intended customers, it might be interrupting them while they're trying to do something else, and so annoy them.

Marketing

> Viral marketing allows companies to inform and persuade consumers, quickly and at very little cost. If people share videos, etc., with their friends, the company reaches lots of potential consumers at no extra cost, like with word-of-mouth advertising.

The **cartoon** is from 2002. At the time of writing, no army has yet sold advertising space on its tanks!

Discussion: Advertising and promotions

This activity has the potential to lead to animated discussion. People tend to assume that everyone else shares their reactions to advertising. For example:

- It is generally argued that cinema advertising, in a dark room with a captive audience, is the most effective.
- Commercials heard on car radios in traffic jams are also hard to ignore.
- When ads interrupt a TV programme you can get up and do something, or change channels – or just sit there and watch them!
- I believe that I don't even notice most ads in newspapers and magazines, but the advertising profession would disagree.
- I find it hard not to notice large advertising posters in the street, but some people genuinely appear not to see them.
- I tend to notice advertising on buses and trains.
- Similarly, I find it hard not to see neon signs, but this doesn't mean they make me buy the brands advertised.
- I have a sign on my mailbox asking people not to put junk mail in it, and I throw away any that does get put in.
- I don't think I've ever bought anything because a flyer was pressed in my hand in the street, but somebody must do: can the entire flyer industry be wrong?
- I never cut out coupons.
- I sometimes impulse-buy things from point-of-sale displays next to checkout counters.
- I'm happy to take free samples and promotional items, but I don't remember ever buying anything as a consequence.
- I will never, ever buy anything that anyone phones me about at home.
- I instantly delete advertising messages that appear on my mobile.
- I don't think I even notice banner ads on web pages. I have a function that blocks pop-ups, and I never read spam.

Irritating ads are unlikely to make you rush out to buy something, but they can plant a brand name in your brain ('Have you seen that infuriating ad for …?'). Ads you find clever or amusing will also stick in your mind, though sometimes you only remember the cleverness or the joke but not the brand name. There is no secret recipe as to what makes an ad both interesting and effective. Some advertising clearly works, but I suspect that hundreds of billions of dollars spent on advertising around the world *are* being wasted.

Listening: Radio commercials
▶ 1.27, 28 29

The learners may be able to answer the first question after one listening. They may need to listen once or twice more to answer the second question, and/or to check their answers in pairs.

> **AUDIO SCRIPT**
>
> 1. Espresso.
>   Espress – oh.
>   Bliss in a cup. Steamed milk on top.
>   You warm my tongue and my soul.
>   Mocha. Latte.
>   Whipped cream and one extra shot.
>   Wake up my senses, for less expenses.
>   High-taste escape, from the rat race.
>   Hand made in front of my eyes.
>   Cappuccino. Americano.
>   Fast, fresh and steamy; man that was easy.
>   Hey Jane, take me to that groovy place called Sheetz.
>   Life is a trip, every day.

2 Typingmaster Pro asks the question, What if you talked like you typed?
What if every time you open-ned your mooth words tumbled out like a le brunch of brokened crockery? How much timme would you wurst back spacing and sprel checking? Would anybody hire youpe? Probably nit. And life would be incredibly fustrating, no doubt. Meybe you should tink five colon backspace comma aboot Typingmaster Pro Typing Tutor for PC and lean how to touch type qickly and measily. Typingmaster Pro hash personalized exercises to target the keys where ou ned more parctice, constantitly monitoring your porgress and adjusting your trainnig. Just lik a good tutor shide, should. So, if you would lik to learn to type as effortgelelessly as you talk, visit us at Typingmaster.com detay option hat symbol seven question mark semi-colon. Typingmaster Pro Typing tutor for PC. Let the typing flop backspace flos backspace flow.

3
Man: I get up, I take a bath, I get dressed, I eat breakfast.
I get up, I take a bath, I get dressed,
Woman: I give him breakfast.
Man: I get up, I take a bath,
Woman: I get him dressed, I give him breakfast.
Man: I get up,
Woman: I give him a bath, I get him dressed, I give him breakfast.
I get him up, I give him a bath, I get him dressed, I give him breakfast.
Narrator: Your life changes quickly. Muscular Dystrophy Association.

ANSWERS AND NOTES

1 The first ad is for 'new coffee house drinks' at Sheetz, which is a chain of several hundred gas stations with convenience stores and coffee shops in six American states. It uses music – a jazz trio with muted trumpet, bass and drums – and a jazz singer, though he's more talking (not even rapping) than singing. The music has the feel of a small jazz club, with the audience regularly applauding and cheering. There are several rhymes and near-rhymes: cup / top, senses / expenses, escape / race, steamy / easy. The ad mentions various different coffees – Espresso, Mocha, Latte, Cappuccino and Americano, and ingredients – steamed milk, whipped cream. Like many ads, it uses hyperbole or exaggeration: the coffee is 'bliss in a cup' that will 'warm [your] soul' and 'wake up [your] senses'. This is typical advertising escapism, but the ad says this explicitly: 'High-taste escape, from the rat race' (though it actually sounds more like 'test' than 'taste'). The ad deliberately uses outdated 1960s hippie slang – 'groovy' and 'life is a trip', though 'trips' were generally associated with illicit drugs rather than coffee. The ad also stresses that the coffees are cheap: 'for less expenses'.

2 The second ad is for Typingmaster Pro, a tutoring program for learning how to touch type. It uses humour: 'What if you talked like you typed?', meaning typed badly, with lots of mistakes. The narrator reads a script full of recognizable words with typing errors, and corrections ('colon, backspace, comma').

Here is a corrected version of the audio script:

Typingmaster Pro asks the question, What if you talked like you typed? What if every time you opened your mouth words tumbled out like a bunch of broken crockery? How much time would you waste back spacing and spellchecking? Would anybody hire you? Probably not. And life would be incredibly frustrating, no doubt. Maybe you should think (five colon backspace comma) about Typingmaster Pro Typing Tutor for PC and learn how to touch type quickly and easily. Typingmaster Pro has personalized exercises to target the keys where you need more practice, constantly monitoring your progress and adjusting your training. Just like a good tutor should. So, if you would like to learn to type as effortlessly as you talk, visit us at Typingmaster.com today. Typingmaster Pro Typing Tutor for PC. Let the typing flow.

3 The third ad is for the American Muscular Dystrophy Association (the MDA). Muscular dystrophy is the collective name for a group of genetic, hereditary diseases that cause progressive weakness and degeneration of the muscles which control movement. The MDA is a voluntary health agency that offers support to people with muscular dystrophy, and sponsors research programmes. The ad aims to raise awareness about muscular dystrophy, and indirectly to raise donations. The ad shows this degeneration by having the man with the disease progressively being able to do less and less, until the woman says she has to do everything for him. It is short and simple, and cleverly uses repetition but with small changes: from 'I get up, I take a bath, I get dressed, I eat breakfast' to 'I get him up, I give him a bath, I get him dressed, I give him breakfast.'

These three ads either won, or were shortlisted for, awards given by the American advertising industry.

Role play: Scripting a radio commercial

This activity could be brainstormed in class, and you might want to accept or reject the learners' suggestions for products or services to advertise before they go any further. The rest of the task – including finding any music or sound effects the learners need – could be done out of class; the learners might need a week or two.

Actually recording the commercial could be done in or out of class, depending on the hardware available, and the learners' level of motivation.

The class (or even other classes) could then be invited to judge which is the best commercial (and, of course, to justify their choice).

Discussion: Successful advertising

Again, learners interested in advertising may have a lot to say, while others may claim not to remember any ads at all. There are no right answers.

An additional question with a mixed or well travelled class would be to ask if advertising tends to be different in different countries.

Here are some **additional questions**, in case time and class interest allow further discussion.

- How many times do you have to see a commercial before it begins to annoy you?

(This is a follow-up to the third question in the **Lead-in**. People have different thresholds of annoyance for repeated commercials.)

- Do you think companies with established brands and products still need to advertise?

(Many tests have shown that companies need to advertise almost continuously in markets in which their competitors are advertising, or they will lose sales. Customer loyalty cannot be taken for granted. In the *Harvard Business Review* survey mentioned above, 72% of respondents agreed that a large reduction in advertising would decrease sales.)

- Do you think that advertising in general presents a true picture of products or services?
- Do you think advertising has a bad influence on children?

(In the *Harvard Business Review* survey, 60% of respondents agreed that advertising does not present a true picture of products, although in many countries, consumer protection legislation has been strengthened since then; and 57% said that it has a bad influence on children.)

- If the best form of advertising is word-of-mouth advertising, you get a lot of free advertising if your brand name becomes a proper noun. For example, lots of English speakers say *Kleenex* instead of tissue, *xerox* instead of photocopy, *hoover* instead of vacuum cleaner, etc. *Hoover* is also used as a verb ('I have to hoover my room').
  - Are there any products like this in your country?
  - This means that a company has achieved excellent brand recognition, but can you think of any *disadvantages* of this for the company?

Other examples of brand names used like this include *sellotape* in Britain and *Scotch tape* in America for sticky tape or adhesive tape, *aspirin* for painkillers, *Band-Aid* instead of adhesive bandage or plaster in America, *Wite-out* in America and *Tipp-Ex* in Britain for correction fluid, and *tupperware* for plastic storage containers for food. People use *to photoshop* as a verb for any computerized editing of photos. Some British people still talk about *biros* for ball-point pens, even if the brand no longer exists. They also mispronounce it: Bíró was the name of the Hungarian inventor, and the original English slogan, which rhymed, was 'Every hero has a biro'!

Disadvantages of this for a company include the fact that if a brand name becomes a common noun and a generic trademark, the company is unable to legally protect its trademark, and loses its intellectual property rights. Customers who buy inferior products from competitors may still think of them as belonging to the producer of the original brand name.

> See also the role play 'Sponsorship' in *Business Roles* by John Crowther-Alwyn, and the simulation 'Advertising Albion' in *Decisionmaker* by David Evans (Cambridge University Press).

14 Banking

This is the first of eight units on finance. It begins with a discussion question that contains most of the basic vocabulary of personal banking. There are texts about the different types of banks and financial institutions, and the credit crisis that began in 2008. There are two listening activities, based on an interview with a recruitment manager at HSBC, and an expert on microfinance in developing countries. The unit ends with a role play about microfinance.

> Additional information about finance is available in *English for the Financial Sector* (Student's Book, Teacher's Book and Audio CD) and *Professional English in Use – Finance*, both available from Cambridge University Press.

Lead-in

The first question covers the major retail banking products and services. Two of the terms are defined (overdraft, mortgage); learners will probably know, or be able to deduce, the meanings of most of the other terms.

The second question is about banking services for business, which are covered in the text which follows.

Reading: Banks and financial institutions

The text defines the different types of financial institutions found both before and after financial deregulation in the 1980s and 90s, and explains why there were strict regulations that could be relaxed. Learners have to insert the names of the different institutions in the text. The text has quite a high vocabulary load, but is followed by vocabulary exercises.

The learners can, of course, check their answers here, and in the vocabulary exercises, in pairs.

> **ANSWERS**
> 1 commercial banks   2 Investment banks
> 3 private banks   4 hedge funds   5 stockbrokers
> 6 Islamic banks   7 non-bank financial intermediaries

Vocabulary

> **ANSWERS**
> 1 1 deposits   2 loan   3 capital   4 stocks or shares   5 bonds   6 merger   7 takeover bid   8 stockbroking   9 portfolio   10 returns   11 bankrupt   12 deregulation   13 conglomerate   14 interest
>
> 2 The following verb–noun combinations are in the text:
> charge interest   do business   give advice
> issue bonds   issue stocks or shares
> make loans   offer advice   offer services
> pass laws   pay interest   provide services
> raise capital   receive deposits   share profits
>
> Other common combinations include:
> make laws   make profits   offer loans   pay a deposit   provide capital   provide loans

Listening 1: Commercial banking

▶ 1.30

> **AUDIO SCRIPT**
>
> **TONY RAMOS**   I think there is a real kind of perception around kind of the world of investment banking and kind of what it offers. I think also as well I think commercial banking, and I guess I would say this as a previous commercial manager, I think is a kind of a best kept secret. I think if you actually and when you do talk to students, when I talk to students and I talk them to about what the commercial banking role is and I talk to them about the fact that you're kind of working in a local marketplace, you're working you know with, like, local entrepreneurs, kind of what the day-to-day job consists of, actually going to see people with their businesses, helping start up those businesses, seeing those businesses

grow and the kind of excitement and the job satisfaction that provides to you, you actually do see their eyes kind of light up and open up, because they kind of think, oh, I actually I didn't think it was about that, I actually thought it was kind of sitting in front of a computer looking at spread sheets, I think it was doing a lot of analysis, it seemed quite dull and stuffy to me.

> **ANSWERS**
> 1 'best kept secret'
> 2 He worked as a commercial bank manager.
> 3 1 local marketplace 2 local entrepreneurs
>   3 going to see 4 helping start up 5 businesses grow
> 4 Sitting in front of a computer looking at spreadsheets, doing a lot of dull analysis

Ask learners which type of financial institution they would like to work for, and why. Some may be persuaded by Tony Ramos as to the interest of commercial banking. Others may dream of working in investment banking. Others, who already know about finance, may have their sights set on hedge funds. And so on.

Reading: The subprime crisis and the credit crunch

Soon after the books mentioned in the box on the previous page were published there was a huge financial crisis. Anyone looking for the recently topical terms *credit crunch* or *toxic debt* or *trash cash* in those books would be disappointed. The real world of finance moves fast. So it seemed necessary to include a text about the subprime crisis in this book. There is no telling what will happen between me writing this and the book being published, or your teaching from it.

Given that much of what happened during the subprime crisis is common knowledge, especially among people interested in finance, your learners may well know about the sequence of events outlined in the text. In which case you could attempt to elicit this information as a **discussion** activity with the books closed before reading the text.

This issue is also the subject of the **Listening** in **Unit 16** on Bonds.

> **ANSWERS**
> 1 Lenders granted mortgages ...
> 2 The mortgage lenders sold ...
> 3 American house prices fell ...
> 4 The value of MBSs fell ...
> 5 Some went bankrupt ...
> 6 There was a credit crisis ...

Vocabulary

> **ANSWERS**
> 1 B 2 C 3 E 4 D 5 A

Discussion

There are no definitive 'right answers' here. As the rubric in the Student's Book suggests, deregulation in the 1980s was a contributing factor. So was the globalization of markets. Some people blame central banks for lowering interest rates in 2000 after the dot-com bubble burst, and again in 2001 after the 9/11 attacks, which led to a fall in the savings ratio. Many people blame the greed of the lenders, the originators of the mortgages, but giving low-income groups the possibility to own their homes is surely a good idea ... if they can afford it. When house prices fell and subprime borrowers defaulted, lenders often repossessed property that was worth less than the amount they had loaned, so they went bankrupt too.

Home buyers were obviously taking risks by buying houses they could scarcely afford, especially if they had 'no down payment' or special low introductory interest rate mortgages. They were hoping house prices would rise, but instead the housing bubble burst, and prices dropped rapidly. Gambling on house prices continuing to increase is rarely a good idea, but people don't seem to learn from history that house-price booms or bubbles invariably burst.

Securitization, including that of risky subprime loans, provides the financial industry with a lot of liquidity, but an industry that has to write off $1,500,000,000,000 (quite apart from provoking much greater losses of

Finance

value on stock markets) doesn't come out looking too clever. Investment banks didn't need to buy subprime mortgages from lenders, securitize them into bonds, and include them in their MBSs and CDOs. One can also blame investors who were willing to purchase MBSs and CDOs because they paid very slightly higher interest than totally safe Treasury bonds.

Some people blame securities rating agencies which gave the MBSs and CDOs high ratings. Since rating agencies receive fees from the creators of securities, it is claimed that they might not adequately assess risks; if they gave lower ratings the issuers of securities might go to a different rating agency.

One can also accuse the US financial regulators of not reacting in time. You can easily find articles on the Internet arguing that the repeal of the Glass-Steagall Act is to blame, as well as articles arguing that this is false.

If you have learners who are particularly knowledgeable about this subject, this activity could be staged as a debate, with groups of students preparing position statements.

Listening 2: Microfinance ▶ 1.31

Some learners may know about microfinance schemes. If not, Anna-Kim Hyun-Seung explains what they are.

The interview with Anna-Kim Hyun-Seung was rerecorded with an actor, for reasons of sound quality. The speaker's accent is more Chinese than Korean.

Anna-Kim Hyun-Seung will reappear in **Units 24** and **25**, talking about corporate social responsibility, and efficiency and employment.

AUDIO SCRIPT

ANNA-KIM HYUN-SEUNG Microfinance schemes started with several NGOs and social enterprises, for example Grameen Bank in Bangladesh. They distribute very small loans to poor people, often without financial collateral. But they use some kind of different collateral, sometimes it can be social collateral, so they create a group of people and within the group people help each other to repay the loan, but it's usually a very small amount of money, and from the bank's point of view it actually provides a unique risk-management tool. Of course, distributing loans to poor people sounds very risky, but because we are talking about a large number of people, with a very small amount of money, it actually creates a very nice portfolio in which the risk can be diversified.

NGOs and social enterprises proved that these kinds of schemes can be scalable, and the poor people are actually repaying the loans, so now the conventional banks like Citibank and Barclays are taking part in these schemes, not for the purpose of doing good only, they are actually doing it as part of their business. They are developing their microfinancing and microcredit products in developing countries. It seems that microfinance is doing really well particularly in Bangladesh and part of India, and there are some positive cases in Latin America and Africa too.

ANSWERS

1 Social collateral – a group of people help each other to repay the loan
2 Making loans to a group of people who can help each other (rather than to individuals)
3 Because the bank makes small loans to a large number of people, which greatly diversifies the risk
4 Because it has been shown that poor people do repay their loans, so microfinance can be part of a normal bank's business
5 Asia, Latin America and Africa

Notes

Collateral is not defined here, but *collateralized* was defined in the previous reading exercise. *NGOs* are non-governmental organizations. Anna-Kim Hyun-Seung uses the word *scalable,* which means an ability to expand or grow; this word is more often used in relation to computing systems than loan portfolios.

Discussion

Given the tone of the Listening extract, few learners are likely to oppose the aims of helping the poor, and at the same time encouraging entrepreneurialism. They might disagree that this is a profitable and risk-free initiative for a bank.

Similar (or at least related) initiatives that learners may know about include socially responsible investment funds; these are discussed in **Unit 16**.

Note

Learners with many (if not most) first languages may be (wrongly) inclined to add a plural *-s* to uncountable collective nouns like *the poor, the rich, the young, the old,* etc.

Role play: Microfinance

There are five role cards at the back of the Student's Book on pages 145, 148, 150, 152 and 153. All four of the main roles B–E are probably necessary to give rise to discussion, i.e. this role play will not work very well if a role is left out in a very small class, though in small groups Director B could also take on Director A's role of chairing the meeting. The meeting could be swayed by any of the four positions, but I suspect that Director E could carry the day if he/she presents his/her case well.

Writing

If the meeting was unable to come to a decision, the minutes would merely record the arguments presented. Looking at the role cards at the back of the Student's Book might help in writing these, if the participants stick to the roles suggested.

> See also the role plays 'Deciding where to invest' and 'Servicing a debt' in *Business Roles 2* by John Crowther-Alwyn, and the simulation 'A Year in Fashion' in *Decisionmaker* by David Evans (Cambridge University Press).

15 Venture capital

This unit contains extracts from an interview with a venture capitalist in Cambridge, a reading exercise about the different elements of a business plan, and a role play about choosing among different investments.

Lead-in

The first question is phrased hypothetically ('If you were starting …'), but of course you may have learners who are running their own company as well as studying, and have already raised capital.

New businesses, or start-ups, are private companies that aren't allowed to sell stocks or shares to the general public. They either operate on money provided by their founders, or get money from venture capital firms, which raise money (venture capital or risk capital or start-up capital) from financial institutions, or occasionally from rich individuals, also known as 'angels' or 'angel investors'.

Established companies are usually able to sell stocks or shares (see **Unit 17**) or issue bonds (see **Unit 16**), or if necessary borrow from banks.

Listening 1: Background experience
▶ 1.32

As his accent reveals, Chris Smart is originally from South Africa. The interview was conducted in an outdoor seating area at the Hotel du Vin in Cambridge (see **Unit 10**), and so is occasionally accompanied by birdsong!

AUDIO SCRIPT

CHRIS SMART   Acacia Capital Partners invests in ICT, Information and Communication Technologies, and that is very broadly based in what is called the technology field, but it doesn't include things like chemistry-based products or materials, or any of those biomedical products, it's purely technology as in IT.
   … so most of the players in the funds have backgrounds in the industries in which they're investing and I mean, I, by hard experience, have, in … run a multi-disciplinary fund, so I did a bit of bio, and a bit of ICT, and I learned very early on that I needed to get somebody into the fund who had the depth of experience in the bio, because I wasn't a bio-scientist. I didn't lose money, but I didn't make the decisions necessary to drive the growth that we wanted, and, you know, you need to have the depth of experience and knowledge in those fields to do it well.

> **ANSWERS**
>
> 1 ICT (Information and Communication Technologies)
> 2 Chemistry-based products or materials, and biomedical products
> 3 He didn't make the right decisions, and had to get somebody into the fund who had experience in the bio field, because you need a lot of experience and knowledge in the fields you invest in.

Listening 2: Investing for ten years
▶ 1.33

AUDIO SCRIPT

CHRIS SMART   OK, so the first thing to recognize is that venture capital is a business in its own right, and venture capitalists are professional in that … and what professional means is they're not investing their own money, they're investing other people's money, so they equally have to raise that money from a market outside, and that in the most general terms is the insurance, it's the insurance industry, so pension funds and insurance companies provide institutional funding to venture capitalists. It is actually a very small percentage, so they will put one to three per cent of their asset base, and no more, into venture capital.
   They raise those on a ten-year cycle, so they have to invest their, the money from a single fund that's been raised on a ten-year cycle, and realize it within the ten years. So on the whole you could say they've got five years to invest, and they've

got five years to reap, but obviously what actually happens is some investments are made in the first couple of years and then might be realized within five years, but other investments, generally after five years there's very little investing happening and most of it is re-investing in the existing portfolio companies and helping them get to a point where they can be sold or listed on a stock market, so you can realize the money.

> **ANSWERS**
>
> 1 1 market outside   2 pension funds   3 insurance companies   4 institutional   5 asset base
> 2 To reap means to get the benefit or profit that is the result of your actions.
> 3 You spend five years investing, and the next five years 'reaping' – getting your money back and making a profit.
> 4 Sometimes you only invest for two years and realize a profit within five years, and sometimes you have to re-invest more money after five years.
> 5 The company should be sold or listed on a stock market (i.e. become a public company with shareholders; see **Unit 17**).

Listening 3: Managing new companies
▶ 1.34

AUDIO SCRIPT

CHRIS SMART   Yes, so one of the things about, certainly the sector we're in which is high-growth, early-stage tech companies, is on the whole the management teams are less experienced, I mean you try and bring in experienced people, but on the whole what you find is that emerging tech areas, the real knowledge is, you know, is vested in people who are still, are coming up, involved in new areas, but in management terms they're inexperienced. So the venture industry as a whole has one major benefit and that is it deals with a lot of these businesses and as a result knows what the challenges are for them, and establishes networks of people that are able to help these businesses. Now that does work well, and it works phenomenally well in the best cases. Equally, I think you'll find very disappointed management in lots of tech companies who say that venture capitalists held out, how much they can contribute and actually they receive very little, so in the end, the management have to deliver, and it is worthwhile if you're on the company side, looking for people that actually have the skills that you want and, you know, might have knowledge in sectors and real experience in comparable companies, and seek them out rather than just simply expect that they can necessarily deliver.

> **ANSWERS**
>
> 1 High-growth, early-stage tech companies
> 2 They are less experienced or inexperienced.
> 3 They know what challenges the companies will face, and have networks of people that can help these businesses.
> 4 Companies should look for people from other companies who have the skills, knowledge and experience they need.

Listening 4: Successes and failures
▶ 1.35

AUDIO SCRIPT

CHRIS SMART   This is, this is the interesting characteristic, I guess, of venture capital in particular, as opposed to private equity, that companies investing in technology have to be failure-tolerant, you have to take some risks in order to get the higher rewards, and on the whole a venture capitalist will set out to achieve, well not to achieve but to expect, a third complete failure of his portfolio, a third will return his money back, and a bit more maybe, and the other third will produce good returns. And from that third that produces good returns, together with the money that you recover from the other third you have to produce a relatively good return on the overall fund, but that's the sort of failure percentage that a normal venture capitalist, an early-stage venture capitalist, will expect, is a third complete failure of their portfolio.

Finance

I think if one looks at the industry statistics, the good returns across the industry are driven by few, very spectacular returns, so, you know, obviously Sequoia with Google has made phenomenal returns, and the Ciscos of the world when they were, you know, succeeded, they made phenomenal returns, the Skypes of the world made phenomenal returns for the likes of Index, so, you know, you have few examples that have made spectacular returns and they actually drive the industry returns …

> **ANSWERS**
> 1 Being 'failure-tolerant'
> 2 He says that a third of the portfolio will fail completely, a third will get you back the money you put in, and maybe a bit more, and a third will produce good returns.
> 3 Google, Cisco and Skype
> 4 Sequoia and Index (actually Index Ventures)

Discussion

Venture capitalists clearly need a thorough knowledge of the industry or industries they invest in, the ability to analyse business plans and financial documents, the ability to communicate with and persuade institutional investors, the ability to accept the fact that some investments lose money (being failure-tolerant), and – perhaps – at least some good luck.

Your learners may feel they potentially possess these attributes, though few are likely to have sufficient experience yet.

Reading: A business plan

> **ANSWERS**
> There are various possibilities, but a standard order might be the following. Certainly numbers 1, 2, 3 and 10 need to be in those positions.
>
> 1 Executive summary   2 Market opportunity
> 3 Product or service   4 Customer profile
> 5 Competition   6 Competitive advantage
> 7 Management team   8 Implementation plan
> 9 Financial analysis   10 Appendix or Appendices

Vocabulary

> **ANSWERS**
> 1 1 competitive advantage   2 sustainable   3 sales forecasts   4 break-even point   5 revenue
>   6 exit strategy   7 founders   8 personnel (or staff)
> 2 1 founders, sales forecasts   2 competitive advantage, sustainable   3 revenue, break-even point   4 personnel (or staff)   5 exit strategy

Role play: Investing in start-ups

This activity is rather abstract (and there are clearly no 'right answers'), but most learners can be expected to have opinions about whether these industries are 'good' (probably clean energy) or 'bad' (possibly nuclear energy, genetically modified food and air travel, even if it is fuel-efficient) – even though this isn't really the focus here – or risky, or whether they offer great potential or are already a little outdated, etc.

In a large class, someone will probably be able to explain, if necessary, what nuclear medical imaging involves – X-rays, MRI (magnetic resonance imaging), CT (computed tomography) scans or CAT (computed axial tomography) scans, etc., and what nanotechnology is. If not, they could do some quick internet research. (Once again, can you remember life *before* Google and Wikipedia!)

Writing

This activity could be done either individually or collaboratively, as a group.

An alternative speaking and writing activity would be to return to the business discussed in **Unit 11** on Products and **Unit 12** on Marketing (juice bar, taxi company, pizza-delivery service, fitness centre, etc.), imagine that it had succeeded and wanted to expand and open branches in other cities, and write a business plan – or rather just an Executive summary, as real business plans are generally over 25 pages long.

This could include short sections outlining the Market opportunity, the Product or service, the Customer profile, and an Implementation plan, as well as a section on Competition that discussed real companies in your city. It would be unlikely to contain a detailed Financial analysis.

Venture capital **Unit 15**

16 Bonds

This unit contains a text explaining bonds, and a listening exercise concerning bonds deriving from mortgage-backed securities, a subject covered in **Unit 14**. There are also texts about different types of bonds, and a case study about selecting among different types of bond funds.

Lead-in and Reading

The Lead-in questions are answered in the text which follows. Briefly:

- Governments can raise taxes and issue bonds.
- Companies can issue both bonds and shares.
- Bond interest is tax-deductible, but unlike share dividends, bond interest payments have to be made, and bonds have to be repaid.
- Bonds are safer than shares for investors, but they generally pay a lower return.

As usual, with relatively small and cooperative classes that might know the answers, you could attempt to elicit the information given in the text as a **discussion** activity with the books closed.

ANSWERS

The following phrases or sentences should be underlined:

- tax revenue
- governments also issue bonds
- they can either issue new shares … on the stock market (equity finance) or borrow money (debt finance), usually by issuing bonds
- bonds are generally safer than stocks or shares, because if an insolvent or bankrupt company sells its assets, bondholders are among the creditors who might get some of their money back
- shares generally pay a higher return than bonds
- bond interest is tax deductible
- dividends paid to shareholders come from already-taxed profits
- debt increases a company's financial risk: bond interest has to be paid
- the principal has to be repaid when the debt matures

Comprehension

ANSWERS

1. False: everyday activities should be financed by cash flows; bonds are usually only issued for expanding a company's activities
2. True
3. True
4. False: bondholders, along with other creditors, may get some of their money back
5. True
6. False: the tax advantage comes from issuing bonds
7. False: systematic public spending should be paid for by tax revenue
8. False: a 5% bond would increase in value if interest rates fell to 4%

Vocabulary

ANSWERS

1. **1** cash flows **2** equity **3** mutual funds **4** pension funds **5** principal **6** maturity **7** coupon **8** insolvent or bankrupt **9** creditors **10** dividends **11** market makers **12** bid or bid price **13** offer or offer price **14** yield
2. The following verb–noun combinations are in the text:

   borrow money, deduct interest payments, finance activities, issue shares, issue bonds, pay (a rate of) interest, pay a (higher) return, pay dividends, pay tax, raise money, receive interest payments, repay principal, sell assets

   Other possible combinations:
   deduct tax, receive dividends, repay bonds, repay money, sell bonds

Finance

Listening: Bonds and subprime mortgages ▶ 2.2

AUDIO SCRIPT

THERESA LA THANGUE Bonds are a very interesting way of raising money. A firm, a listed firm has two routes to raising capital. One is through debt and one's through equity. Equity is when they sell off shares in the market, and then you have debt where they'll go to a large, usually a large bank and say 'We'd like to raise X billion dollars,' and they will be sold a bond by that organization. Now most bonds are rated by the credit rating agencies. The governments do it as well and their bonds tend to be Triple A [AAA] rated, they are the 'gold standard' of bonds. And most firms that issue bonds in London they'll be Triple A [AAA] rated or Triple B [BBB] rated by the various credit rating agencies.

Now what happened in America with mortgage-backed securities, which as I said before were a very good bond, and they were considered to be a very safe investment because mortgages are long term and they tend to be solid. What happened in the States was a number of organizations had mortgages from subprime lenders who are considered to be more risky – they have bad credit history, or they have large mortgages against properties which they couldn't really afford, and what was happening in the US was that bonds were being packaged that were partly good debt, good safe secure debt, and partly this very bad debt. But the credit rating agencies didn't look too closely, it would appear, at what was happening, and had given all of these bonds Triple A [AAA] ratings.

What happens with a bond, it's then securitized, where the person, the firm that holds the bond then chops it up into small pieces and sells those small pieces on, so basically they're selling on the debt, and it's a huge market and it usually works extremely well. The problem with securitizing, of the mortgage-backed securities in the US, is that each little bit of security got a little bit of the good debt, but also a little bit of the bad debt, and these were sold off, and the bad debt is going bad, and nobody is quite sure if the bits of securities they've bought are going to go bad, or if they have gone bad, or if they've got lots of bad, and this is the problem at the moment, that nobody really trusts each other's balance sheet, so they're not, so the banks aren't lending to each other.

ANSWERS

1. AAA (Triple A) (the official rating) and 'gold standard', meaning very safe, as safe as gold
2. Because mortgages are long term and they tend to be 'solid', i.e. safe, as traditionally they were only lent to people who would be able to repay them
3. People with a bad credit history, or with large mortgages against properties which they couldn't really afford. (She says 'subprime lenders', but although there were institutions which lent these mortgages, the description applies to subprime *borrowers*.)
4. Mortgages were securitized: packaged into bonds containing partly safe debt and partly very bad debt.
5. They didn't correctly analyse the mortgage-backed securities and gave them all AAA ratings.
6. Investors in mortgage-backed securities, particularly banks, didn't know if they had good or bad debt, and no longer trusted each other's accounts (balance sheets) and so they stopped lending to each other.

Discussion

Banks in most non-'Anglo-Saxon' countries tend *not* to lend mortgages to people who show little sign of being able to repay them, yet banks in many countries *did* buy American subprime mortgage-backed securities.

Reading: How to profit from bonds

The three texts are extracted and slightly edited from:
- Rush to buy government bonds, by Julia Kollewe, *The Guardian*, 6 March 2009
  http://www.guardian.co.uk/business/2009/mar/06/bankofenglandgovernor-interest-rates
- Corporate bonds: the only 'hot' story in town, by Julian Knight, *The Independent*, 11 January 2009
  http://www.independent.co.uk/money/spend-save/corporate-bonds-the-only-hot-story-in-town-1299060.html

- Why high-yield bonds are only for the brave: Lending your money to struggling companies can be lucrative, by Rob Griffin, *The Independent*, 28 March 2009 http://www.independent.co.uk/money/spend-save/why-highyield-bonds-are-only-for-the-brave-1655993.html (consulted March 2009).

> **ANSWERS**
>
> 1 British government bonds (or gilts); (investment-grade) corporate bonds; high-yield (non-investment-grade) corporate bonds
> 2 The British government is buying back billions of pounds' worth of gilts, which increases their price (by the logic of supply and demand); because of the recession, companies are having to pay investors high interest rates to convince them to buy (investment-grade) bonds; the interest rates paid by risky, non-investment-grade bonds are extremely high
> 3 To inject money into the depressed economy (to 'kickstart' it)
> 4 Companies that are considered to have a reasonable chance of going bust and defaulting on their loans
> 5 Some of the companies might default, but a careful selection of high-yield bonds reduces the investor's risk.

Vocabulary

> **ANSWERS**
>
> 1 soared (to soar)   2 to kickstart   3 benchmark
> 4 slump, recession, depression   5 rally
> 6 defaulting (to default)   7 to go bust

Note

The **cartoon** has an employee of a fund management company suggesting that they re-brand a fund that is doing very badly as one designed specifically for people with low self-esteem! Self-esteem (or at least esteem) was mentioned in **Unit 2** in relation to McGegor's Theory Y and Maslow's 'hierarchy of needs'.

Discussion

At the time of writing (May 2009), most people expect the credit crunch to end and the global economy to revive within 18 months or so. There is, of course, no way of knowing whether this will come to pass.

Under normal circumstances, the increase in gilt prices would only be temporary; once the government had stopped buying them back, their price would fall to a more usual level. Besides, the higher the price of a fixed-income bond, the lower its yield.

After a recession, corporate bond interest rates should fall again, so the price of existing long-term bonds paying high interest rates would remain high. Once high-quality bond rates fell, the rates paid by non-investment-grade bonds would fall too, although this also depends on how many of them defaulted.

Case study: Investing in funds

You may want to have the learners read this page, perhaps out of class, before they discuss the funds, so they can look up or ask about any vocabulary they don't know.

Here are some notes about the different funds:
1 Although the renewable energy industry does indeed have a high rate of growth, there is no guarantee that the small firms which lead the global market today will continue to do so.
2 Although it true that emerging markets account for one-third of global economic activity and three-quarters of growth, and have a strong competitive advantage as manufacturing locations, the fund can obviously only invest in a small selection of countries, markets and companies. Even if debt securities issued by governments are safe, there is always the risk of losing money due to changes in exchange rates. Debts from institutions and companies in emerging markets may be less secure than those issued by major institutions and companies in developed markets.
3 There is nearly always a correlation between a high yield (or rate of return) and risk, and this fund is honest enough to state that 'considerable fluctuations in price cannot be ruled out.' 'Non-investment-grade bonds' means bonds with a low

credit rating (as opposed to investment-grade bonds with AAA ratings, etc.), so there are clearly big risks involved here.

4 The claim that prestigious branded luxury goods with high prices enjoy stable demand even during tough economic times is dubious: it depends on quite how bad the situation gets. Even if new markets for luxury goods are opening up in emerging markets, investing solely in this branch is probably risky.

5 The ethical growth fund gives more information about companies it does *not* invest in than about companies in which it does. It makes no specific claims apart from aiming to achieve the highest possible capital growth. It is certainly possible to achieve capital growth by investing in ethical companies (even if this growth might be less than that offered by less ethical investments), but there is no guarantee that this fund will select the best opportunities. (There is more on socially responsible investment and corporate social responsibility in **Unit 24**.)

6 As mentioned in the previous unit, the vast majority of microfinance clients repay their loans. The argument that their small-scale local businesses are generally unaffected by developments in global markets is probably a good one, and investing in this fund would almost certainly constitute diversification for most investors. The fund only aims to realize a return that is (slightly?) higher than the investor could get by buying money market funds (which generally pay more than deposit accounts in banks but less than bonds), which is probably achievable.

7 This fund invests in both medium and high quality debt securities, but they are all inflation-linked. The fund states that it invests worldwide, in accordance with the principle of risk-spreading, but it does not specify if the investments are all in euros, or whether exchange rate risks might be involved.

8 This fund, like any fund called 'dynamic', is clearly taking risks in the search for high earnings – 'Investments are made globally with no restrictions as to country, currency or sector ... across the entire range of borrower ratings and maturities.' But it is honest, pointing out that 'Sizeable short-term price fluctuations are possible.' This does suggest, however, that the fund managers are confident that their fund will grow in the long term. But as the famous quote from John Maynard Keynes has it, 'In the long run we are all dead' (*A Tract on Monetary Reform* (1923) Chapter 3).

A *Eurobond* is an international bond that is denominated in a currency other than that of the country where it is issued.

Writing

This report could easily include relevant phrases or sentences from the advertisements in the Student's Book.

See also the simulation 'Wall Street Blues' in *Decisionmaker* by David Evans (Cambridge University Press).

17 Stocks and shares

This unit has a jumbled text explaining stocks and shares; listening and vocabulary exercises practising the verbs and expressions people use to talk about rises and falls in asset prices; an extract from a book about the work of an analyst in an investment bank; and a role play involving investing money in a stock portfolio.

Lead-in

Here's a wholly fictitious story that could be used to introduce the opening discussion task:

> Do you know how Rockefeller made his first million dollars? One day, when he was young and very poor, he was walking along the street and he found a one cent piece. He bought an apple with it, polished it on his shirt, made it look nice and shiny, and sold it for two cents. Then he bought two apples, polished them, and sold them both for two cents each, and so on. After two months, he had enough money to buy a barrow for his apples. After two years, he was just about to open his first fruit store ... when he inherited a million dollars from his uncle! This is still the quickest way to get rich.

By way of answers to the question about advantages and disadvantages:

- Putting your money under the mattress is probably not a good idea unless you live in a country with banks that are likely to go bankrupt, no investment opportunities, no inflation, and no burglaries, fires, burst pipes, landslides, earthquakes, etc.
- Winning the lottery would probably give you the best possible return on your money, but the odds against winning are generally enormous (e.g. about 14 million to 1 for the top prize in the British lottery).
- About one gambler out of eight comes away from Las Vegas or Monte Carlo with a profit.
- Keeping your money in a bank is generally safe, although interest rates paid to depositors are generally lower than those on the money markets, the bond market, etc.
- The price of gold sometimes rises dramatically – for example during financial crises, such as at the time of writing – but it can also fall. Furthermore, it pays no interest, and it costs money to store gold in safety.
- Buying a painting gives you something to look at, but also something to protect against damage and insure against theft (though people who buy paintings as investments often keep them in bank vaults). Prices of Impressionist and post-Impressionist paintings have risen dramatically in the past 40 years, but they could also fall.
- Property (BrE) or real estate (AmE) usually appreciates in value in the long term, but the property market is subject to speculative booms and slumps, so you have to buy at the right time. But Mark Twain's advice, 'Buy land, young man, they're not making it any more,' is probably still valid.
- Government bonds and bonds in secure companies are generally a safe investment, but a long-term fixed-interest bond can lose a lot of value if interest rates rise sharply. As discussed in **Unit 16**, bonds including subprime mortgages were at the heart of the financial crisis that began in 2008.
- Shares are more risky than bonds, as their value can fluctuate wildly (e.g. minus 30% in three days in the crash of October 1987, minus 45% in autumn 2008, etc.), and because there is no guarantee of receiving a dividend, unlike bond interest payments.
- Investing in a hedge fund is not open to everybody: many funds require a minimum investment of $500,000 or more. The whole point of hedge funds is that they are supposed to be able to make money in a bear market, but this doesn't always work.
- The advantages of giving your money away are obvious: no more worries about income tax, capital gains tax, capital transfer tax, bank charges, accountants, complicated tax returns, no more worrying about the S&P Index while you are on holiday (as in the cartoon in the Student's Book), etc.!

Reading: Stocks and shares

This text explains the basics of stocks and shares: why and how they are issued, how they are traded, etc. It is not followed by a vocabulary exercise because many of the sentences are themselves definitions of words. The text also includes vocabulary that appears in the following exercises (e.g. *bear market*, *stock index*).

Obviously learners who already know something about stocks and shares will find this exercise easier than those who don't, but most business learners can be expected to have some knowledge of the subject. As always, if you expect your learners to be familiar with most of the content of the text, you could also try to elicit the information first as a question and answer activity.

> **ANSWERS**
>
> 1 J   2 D   3 A   4 F   5 G   6 C   7 K   8 E   9 I
> 10 H   11 L   12 B

Discussion

1   It is self-evident that the *majority* of market participants cannot regularly outperform the market, but there are a few famous investors who do (such as Warren Buffett, George Soros, etc.). The armies of analysts working for investment banks – who are roundly ridiculed in Geraint Anderson's book *Cityboy*, excerpted below – exist because the industry believes that there are ways to beat the market (by having more information than other people). What your learners believe may depend on what books they have read, or what their finance professors have told them.

The **cartoon** about prices falling suggests that stock prices are based on (possibly irrational) fears rather than on economic reality. This means that one could have a more accurate view of a company's real value than the one reflected in its market price, but this information would only become valuable when or if the rest of the market took into account the real economic facts.

2   A person revealing privileged information (only known to some people in the company) in this way would probably be guilty of breaking company rules, while anyone selling shares on this information would be guilty of insider trading, which is against the law. Whether you feel you should help friends by revealing such information, and whether they should expect you to do so, depends on your individual ethics, and on whether you are what the Dutch intercultural theorist Fons Trompenaars called a universalist or a particularist: see **Unit 4**.

3   There are two basic ways to make money from falling stock markets. One is with *put options*, which are explained in **Unit 18**; the other is by *short-selling*, which is explained in the reading text which follows.

Listening: A financial news report

▶ 2.3

AUDIO SCRIPT

NEWSREADER   Here in New York, the Dow-Jones is down –58.86 points at 7,123.22, a drop of –0.82%, and the S&P 500 has drifted a little more to 742.55, that's down –0.37%. But the NASDAQ Composite is slightly firmer at 1,397.04, that's up 0.4%. Things weren't much better in Europe today, with the DAX in Frankfurt tumbling 2.61%, and the CAC-40 in Paris continuing its slide, finishing –1.83% lower. In London the Footsie 100 kissed goodbye to 2.5%.

It wasn't all doom and gloom in Asia though, with the Nikkei 225 in Tokyo climbing to 7,568.42, that's a gain of 1.48%. In Australia, the S&P/ASX 200 is virtually unchanged at 3,344.50.

Over on the currency markets, the dollar's lost 0.0048 cents against the euro this morning, and 0.0015 against the pound, now trading at a dollar 43, while it's steady against the yen, adding a tiny 0.00001 cents – I've never even seen one of those! – trading at $0.0102.

Over on commodities, gold is back where it started this morning, at $942, while oil's been yo-yoing, but right now it's on 43.60, that's a dollar 46 more than this time yesterday.

ANSWERS	
The Dow-Jones	Fallen
The S&P 500	Fallen
The NASDAQ	Risen
Shares in Germany	Fallen
Shares in France	Fallen
Shares in Britain	Fallen
Shares in Japan	Risen
Shares in Australia	Unchanged
The dollar against the euro	Fallen
The dollar against the pound	Fallen
The dollar against the yen	Unchanged
Gold	Unchanged
Oil	Risen

Vocabulary

The idioms chosen here and in the **Listening** are just a few of those regularly used by financial journalists. Interested learners should be encouraged to read the market reports in newspapers such as the *Financial Times*, *Wall Street Journal*, or *International Herald Tribune*, or watch the financial programmes on CNN, CNBC, Bloomberg, etc.

> **ANSWERS**
>
> **1** C **2** E **3** C **4** A **5** D **6** E **7** D **8** A
> **9** B **10** C **11** E **12** B

Reading: Hedge funds

The text is from *Cityboy: Beer and Loathing in the Square Mile* by Geraint Anderson (London: Headline, 2008), pp. 140–141.

Some **additional questions** might be: has anyone done anything similar (written exposés of the financial sector) in the learners' countries? Would anyone doing so lose their job if their identity was discovered? Is it hypocritical to write a column condemning investment banking while continuing to work as an analyst and earning huge bonuses?

In this extract, Anderson summarizes one of the major strategies of hedge funds, namely short-selling. As mentioned in the Student's Book, hedge funds are private investment funds which use a lot of derivative instruments in the search for higher returns; consequently they are considered in more detail in **Unit 18** on **Derivatives**.

The questions are quite difficult, in that the first one requires background knowledge (but knowledge that most learners can be expected to have), and the second and third involve implied meanings.

BACKGROUND NOTES

Cityboy is a salacious and wonderfully funny account of the working life of an analyst in investment banks in the City of London. Anderson – a former hippy and Cambridge history student, and the son of a former Labour MP – previously wrote an anonymous newspaper column about life in the City, and turned it into a book when he stopped working there. The book's subtitle is a clear reference to Hunter S. Thompson's autobiographical novel *Fear and Loathing in Las Vegas: A Savage Journey to the Heart of the American Dream* (1972).

> **SUGGESTED ANSWERS**
>
> 1 The 'tech bubble' is also often called the 'dot-com boom' or the 'dot-com bubble': the rapid, speculative rise and even more rapid fall of the price of internet company stocks between 1995 and 2001. A 'bubble' means prices which rise and fall a great deal in a short period of time.
>
> 2 'Boy' suggests youth and immaturity – after all, most of the people working in finance are adults – but also excessively competitive, testosterone-fuelled, masculine, 'alpha male' behaviour. (There is also an expression common in London, 'wide boy', meaning a working-class male who lives by his wits and wheeling and dealing, and a common prejudice – or a realization? – that the City is full of such people.)
>
> 3 This suggests that the entire industry of financial experts and analysts is trying to say clever-sounding things that actually have little meaning, in order to sound like specialists and thereby earn a living.
>
> 4 Shorting shares means borrowing shares from a fund or company that isn't planning to sell them in the short term, selling them, waiting for their price to fall, and then buying them back at a lower price and returning them to their original owner.
>
> 5 The investment banks had to encourage their analysts and brokers to spend more time working with hedge funds than with their traditional institutional clients because they make money from each transaction and the hedge funds were making many more transactions than traditional clients.

Unit 17 Stocks and shares

Role play: Investing a client's money

The longer the learners hold their imaginary portfolio, the more chance there is of it increasing or decreasing in value. This is therefore not an activity to undertake at the end of a course. Lists of the most important stocks (and sometimes complete lists) in major stock markets are printed in the financial pages of serious newspapers, and of course on the Internet. It would be helpful (or indeed necessary) to find a list of recently floated companies, as the instructions request the learners to select two of these. Financial sections of newspapers also usually list the exchange-traded funds issued by banks and mutual funds, and bond prices.

With more motivated students, another possibility is to allow them to buy and sell during the period that the portfolio is in existence, charging, say, 2% commission for each transaction. After they have established their portfolios (and during the following weeks, if the portfolios can be changed) the learners can be invited to explain the reasons for the positions they have taken. At the chosen end date, the learners can present their results, and attempt to provide reasons or explanations for them.

18 Derivatives

This unit contains vocabulary and comprehension exercises about financial derivatives, a listening about hedge funds and structured products, a text from the *Times Online* website about financial spread-betting, and a closing exercise drawing together all the financial instruments discussed in **Units 16–18**.

Lead-in

The newspaper headlines in the Student's Book reveal that *derivatives* seems to collocate with *losses*. The claim by the American investor Warren Buffett that derivatives are 'Financial weapons of mass destruction' is outlined in an article in Unit 19 of *English for the Financial Sector* (Cambridge University Press).

> ANSWERS
> - The main types of derivatives are futures, options and swaps.
> - Derivatives are used for hedging (protection against price changes) and speculating (buying or selling assets, hoping to make a profit in the future).
> - They are risky because there is no limit to how much the value of the underlying asset can change, leaving the possibility of huge losses on the derivative instrument.
> - The headlines refer to the following cases:
>   - Barings Bank in London, which went bankrupt when a single trader lost $1.4bn on unauthorized stock index futures in 1995
>   - Daiwa Bank in Japan, which lost $1.1bn through unauthorized bond trading in 1995
>   - the US hedge fund Long Term Capital Management, which lost $4.6bn on derivative trading in 1998
>   - the Allied Irish Bank, which lost $697m on unauthorized currency trading in 2002
>   - Société Générale in France, which lost €4.9bn on a single trader's unauthorized stock index futures in 2008.
> - Other examples include:
>   - Sumitomo Bank in Japan, which lost $2.6bn on unauthorized copper trades in 1996
>   - BAWAG in Austria, which lost $2.4bn on unauthorized currency trading in 2006
>   - the French bank Crédit Agricole, which lost €250m on a single trader's unauthorized bets on credit markets in 2007

> - Caisse d'Epargne in France, which lost €600m on unauthorized equity derivatives trading in 2008. An internet search for 'derivatives losses' will turn up others.
> - Warren Buffett has made his money by what he calls 'value investing' – buying shares that appear to be underpriced by some forms of fundamental analysis, rather than by speculating in derivatives. Only time will tell whether derivatives will have brought down the global financial system before you read this! Given that individual derivative losses can run into billions of dollars, Buffett may have a point.

Vocabulary: Derivatives

> ANSWERS
> **1** F **2** A **3** E **4** D **5** C **6** B **7** H **8** G

Discussion

These questions require not only an understanding of the terms in the previous Vocabulary exercise, but an understanding of how derivatives can be used. Many business learners will know about derivatives from finance courses. All the information required to answer is given below.

> ANSWERS
> 1 The obvious answer would be to arrange a futures contract: the producer gets a fixed future selling price, and the buyer gets a fixed buying price.
> 2 The company could try to arrange an interest rate swap with a company with floating rate debt that expected interest rates to rise.

> 3 Buy a put option giving the right to sell the stock in the future at the current market price. (See also the notes below.)
> 4 Buy a call option giving the right to buy the stock in the future at the current price. (See also the notes below.)
> 5 In all the contracts suggested in the previous answers, one party wins and the other loses. Futures, options and swaps are a 'zero-sum game': one party's gains are equal to the other party's losses. This is unlike mutually beneficial 'win–win situations', which is what all business books say negotiations and business partnerships should be.

Notes

1 If the price of cocoa does change before the date of the futures contract, either the producer or the buyer will have lost money by signing the contract.
2 If interest rates do fall, the company exchanging its floating rate notes will lose.
3 If the stock price falls, the seller of the put option will lose.
4 If the stock price rises, the seller of the call option will lose. In the contrary situations, the seller (also known as the writer) of the options will earn the price of the option, the premium, as the option will not be exercised.

Consequently, alternative answers (which learners with a knowledge of options may suggest) would be:

3 Write (i.e. sell) a call option giving someone else the right to *buy* the share; if the market price of the underlying security remains below the option's strike price (or exercise price: the agreed-upon price at which the option can be exercised), the buyer will not take up the option, and the seller earns the premium.
4 Write (i.e. sell) a put option giving someone else the right to *sell* the share; if the market price of the underlying security remains above the strike price, the buyer will not take up the option, and the seller earns the premium.

Listening: Hedge funds and structured products ▶ 2.4

Teresa La Thangue appeared in **Unit 16**, talking about bonds and subprime mortgages.

AUDIO SCRIPT

THERESA LA THANGUE Now hedge funds, it's a very, it's a term that covers a number of organ-… ways of trading. They tend to be things that only firms, or very wealthy organizations, can invest in. In the UK, there is no retail access to hedge funds because we believe that at the moment, hedge funds don't do enough to ensure that retail investors would be aware of the risks, what they were getting involved with.

Hedge funds used to be, many, many years ago when they first became popular, just a way of hedging your bets, so if you had a derivative you would buy another product, a smaller product, to go against the risk involved with the derivative. But now they are seen as an investment tool in their own right, and they can invest in anything, and they do, they invest in, some of them are just straight equity investors, where they invest in the price of a share going up, some of them are short-sellers, some of them are very involved in spread-betting, some involved very much in the derivatives market, some will invest in bonds, so it's basically just a bit of a cover-all term now.

A structured product is pretty much similar to a hedge fund, though I understand that if you are making available to the retail community a structured product, it must have a very consistent risk profile across it, so you don't find that you're investing in a bond, a Triple A bond, but also a very risky derivative at the other end, so you must have a very consistent risk profile so that you, the … the structured product that you buy, is consistent with your understanding of risk.

> ### ANSWERS
> 1 Because the FSA (Financial Services Authority), which regulates the financial industry in Britain, doesn't think that hedge funds would adequately warn retail investors about the risks involved in investing in a hedge fund

2 They are no longer just a way of hedging your positions (or 'bets'); they are an investment tool, a way of investing in equities, bonds, derivatives, doing spread-betting, etc.
3 Buying equities, short-selling, spread-betting, derivatives, bonds
4 Structured products offered by banks must have a very consistent risk profile (i.e. not be a mixture of safe and risky elements).

Notes

Short-selling was explained in **Unit 17**; *spread-betting* is explained in the reading text which follows.

Reading: Spread-betting

The text is a shortened version of an article that appeared on the *Times Online* website called 'Ten things to know about spread-betting' http://www.timesonline.co.uk/tol/money/investment/article 1305642.ece (consulted March 2009).

ANSWERS
1 'taking a punt'
2 'the odds are in the spread-betting company's favour' and 'that's if you make any profits, of course'
3 Not necessarily; although there is no limit as to how high a stock price, commodity price or stock index could rise, it cannot fall below zero (but zero is a long way below the example quoted – 5,016 points for the FTSE, at £10 a point). Furthermore, the article says you can establish 'stop-loss' limits.
4 No; the final example is about hedging: protecting the value of a fund tracking a stock index

Discussion: Investing, speculating and gambling

Notes

There are no definitively 'right answers' here, but:
- Buying **stocks or shares** can be a simple investment, but buying them with money you cannot really afford, hoping their price will soon rise, is clearly speculation.
- Buying **bonds** is generally considered to be a safe investment, but buying them in the hope of forthcoming falls in interest rates is clearly speculation.
- Buying foreign **currency** to use in the future is essentially speculation; if you didn't expect the exchange rate to move unfavourably, why buy now? Over 90% of the trades on foreign exchange markets are speculative, unrelated to real needs such as travel or purchasing imports.
- **Futures** are often used to hedge, i.e. to protect against losses, but one can also trade in security, commodity or financial futures as a form of speculation. Given that futures contracts have to be exercised, this might also be thought of as gambling, e.g. buying 100 tonnes of copper because you expect to be able to sell it easily is a serious gamble if you end up paying much more than the market price when the contract ends, and can't sell it.
- Buying call or put **options** to buy or sell stocks in the future can either be hedging (protecting an investment) or speculation (especially if one does not possess the underlying shares). But since either the buyer or the seller of an option is guaranteed to lose money, options could fairly be categorized as either speculation or gambling, depending on one's point of view.
- Similarly with **swaps**: if one party wins, the other has to lose. This might be thought of as either speculation or gambling.
- **Structured products** usually involve a combination of assets, and often only make a profit if certain market conditions are met (stock market prices, interest rates, exchange rates, etc.). There is by definition a risk, even though, as Teresa La Thangue says, there must be a consistent and understandable risk profile. This is clearly speculation at the very least; some may think of it as gambling.

Role play: Financial instruments

There are three question cards at the back of the Student's Book on pages 145, 148 and 150. The learners need to be divided into trainers and trainees. The trainees should look at one of the three sets of questions at the back of the Student's Book, and think about the questions, either individually or in pairs or small groups; give them a few minutes to decide on their answers. The trainers could also work in pairs or groups, deciding what the correct answers are. The teacher needs to check that the trainers know the right answers, by asking them (out of the hearing of the trainees), and showing them the correct answers below if necessary (the answers may be photocopied). The roles can be reversed or the pairs or groups changed after the first or second question card, though it is preferable to have stronger learners taking the trainer's role. A simpler alternative would be to have the teacher play the role of trainer.

Writing

The training memo or information leaflet would include the information in the answers below, perhaps with an introductory sentence such as 'This leaflet explains the income investors can receive from bonds,' or 'This page lists the ways in which investors and institutions can make money from stocks or shares.'

ANSWERS

Questions (1)
1 Regular interest payments, paid six-monthly or annually
2 They can buy futures contracts, as well as options that they only need to exercise if prices move in the right direction.
3 They can sell the index in a spread-betting market.

Questions (2)
1 Annual dividends, although the company is not obliged to pay these. If the company retains its profits without investing them, the money is recorded in the Balance Sheet as 'shareholders' equity', showing that it still belongs to the shareholders, even if it has not been distributed.
2 Market interest rates go up and down depending on the economic situation and decisions made by central banks (see Unit 23), but fixed interest bonds continue to pay the same rate. Successful companies are able to issue bonds at relatively low rates; companies in financial difficulties, or in danger of going bankrupt, have to pay much higher rates.
3 The yield of a bond depends on the price paid for it; bonds may be sold either above or below their 'par value' or 'nominal value' – the price written on them – depending on interest rate fluctuations, or the financial situation of the issuer.

4 Companies can buy currency or interest rate futures, or arrange interest rate swaps and currency swaps with other companies; investors can buy currency or interest rate futures.

Questions (3)
1 Investors can buy shares and sell them later if the price goes up. They can buy call options to buy shares at a fixed price in the future; if the price rises they can exercise the option, and buy and sell the shares at a profit. If they possess shares, they can buy a put option to sell them at a particular price, and potentially make a profit if the market price is lower than the option's strike price (though this is more often a way of cutting losses than making a capital gain).
2 They can sell call and put options, and earn the premium if the options are not exercised (because the market price went in the opposite direction from that anticipated by the buyer).
3 Hedge funds can short-sell shares they do not possess, if they are able to borrow them from a fund that has a long position in the shares.

English for Business Studies, Third Edition
© Cambridge University Press 2010

19 Accounting and financial statements

Bookkeeping and accounting – recording transactions, elaborating budgets, calculating costs and expenses, preparing financial statements and tax returns, and so on – are central to all commercial activity, from the smallest sole-trader or self-proprietorship (one-person business) to the largest multinational company. Financial control is equally crucial for all non-commercial organizations and institutions.

This unit aims to introduce the basic concepts and terminology of accounting and financial statements. It begins with exercises defining basic accounting terminology and the different areas of accounting. There is a listening exercise in which a university lecturer explains the difficulty of valuing assets. There are exercises and a role play based on Google's financial statements.

Business students are likely to have followed courses in accounting early in their studies, or even at secondary school, and so will probably be able to launch straight into the **Lead-in** and the **Vocabulary** exercises. There is a lot of vocabulary work in this unit, but a lot of vocabulary is necessary to begin to discuss any aspect of accounting.

If you require further background information on accounting, you might find Units 2 to 17 of *Professional English in Use – Finance* (Cambridge University Press) helpful.

Lead-in

The skills required for bookkeeping are probably accuracy and concentration, and some mathematical (or at least arithmetical) ability. Managerial or management and cost accounting require analytical ability and mathematical competence. Tax accounting requires a thorough knowledge of tax laws and accounting combined with a desire to help clients reduce their tax liabilities. Auditing requires strong analytical skills, and honesty; 'creative accounting' presumably requires the same, with the substitution of dishonesty for honesty.

The **cartoon** seems to show an attempt to take the practice known as creative accounting (defined in the second **Vocabulary** exercise), also known as 'window dressing', to an even higher level!

Vocabulary

> ANSWERS
> 1 1 B   2 B   3 B   4 A   5 C   6 C   7 A   8 B
>   9 A   10 A
> 2 1 cost accounting   2 tax accounting
>   3 auditing   4 accounting   5 managerial or management accounting   6 'creative accounting'   7 bookkeeping
> 3 1 C   2 A   3 B

> 4 The most likely collocations are: calculate liabilities, calculate taxes, keep records, pay liabilities, pay taxes, receive income, record expenditure, record income, record transactions, value assets, value liabilities

There is a discussion question in the middle of these vocabulary exercises. People studying business degrees are likely to find mere bookkeeping beneath them. Managerial or management accounting implies having a somewhat higher position in a company. I have yet to meet a learner who wanted to be a cost accountant, and few who are already thinking about tax accounting or creative accounting. In fact my experience of business students is that in their first year most of them say they want to work in marketing ('because it's creative'), but in their final year they enthusiastically apply for jobs with the big auditing firms.

Notes

The term *Balance sheet* is used in both Britain and the US; the alternative name *Statement of financial position* is also used in the US. The name *Income statement* is used in the US, and according to International Financial Reporting Standards. The name *Profit and loss statement* is also used, while *Profit and loss account* is also used in Britain.

Finance

The name *Cash flow statement* (or *Statement of cash flows*) has largely replaced the names *Funds flow statement, Statement of funds flows, Source and application of funds statement* and *Statement of changes in financial position*.

British company law also requires companies to produce a fourth statement, a *Statement of total recognized gains and losses* or *STRGL*, showing any gains and losses that are not included in the profit and loss account, such as the revaluation of fixed assets.

Reading 1: Google Inc. Balance sheet

Financial statements such as these can be found in a company's Annual Reports, and by searching for the company on financial websites such as http://www.google.com/finance, http://moneycentral.msn.com/home.asp, http://finance.yahoo.com, http://www.reuters.com/finance, etc.

> **ANSWERS**
> 1 **1** Shareholders' Equity **2** Intangibles **3** Additional Paid-In Capital **4** Accrued Expenses **5** Total Receivables **6** Accounts Payable **7** Prepaid Expenses **8** Retained Earnings **9** Property/Plant/Equipment **10** Goodwill **11** Total Liabilities
> 2 Total Assets, and Total Liabilities & Shareholders' Equity
> 3 $1,404.11 million (the Prepaid Expenses)
> 4 The capital the shareholders have paid into the company (Common Stock + Additional Paid-In Capital + Other Equity) = $14,677.24 million, which is greater than the Retained Earnings ($13,561.63 million).
> 5 The money Google owed at the balance sheet date was $2,302.09 million (Total Current Liabilities), which is less than what it was owed: $2,642.19 million (Total Receivables, Net).

Listening: Valuing assets ▶ 2.5

AUDIO SCRIPT

RICHARD BARKER So, a company's balance sheet, in principle, is intended to give you the value of the company's business, but in practice, some assets are very easy to value, and some are very difficult to value. So if you hold some shares in another company or something, or you hold some money in a bank account, this is very easy to value. On the other hand, if your assets comprise research and development, or people for that matter, then it's in principle very difficult to put a value on those things. And when you measure the profit of a company, what you're trying to do is measure a change in value, so the difference between what a company is worth at the beginning of a year, and what it is worth at the end of a year, is the profit that it makes, or the loss that it makes. And if it's difficult to measure the value of assets in the first place, it's also difficult to measure whether a company's making profit or not.

So an example might be ... take an airport, and a runway on an airport. Well, what's a runway worth? would be one question. You could estimate that maybe, you could estimate how long you think the airport will operate for, how many planes will land on it, what the value of one airport will be, what the value of Heathrow would be in comparison with the value of Gatwick, for example. But it's actually quite a subjective thing to measure. And then you've got to figure out, well, how long is this thing going to last, because every year you want to take the depreciation on that runway and charge it against profit – you want to take a reduction in the value of the runway, and if you think the runway will last 25 years, then you will depreciate it four times as quickly as if you think it will last 100 years. So there's lots of estimation and judgement in accounting because the value of an asset depends upon the future uncertain events, and those uncertain events, by their very nature, can't be estimated very easily.

> **ANSWERS**
>
> 1 Research and development, people, and an airport runway
> 2 The difference between what a company is worth at the beginning and the end of a year
> 3 Because you don't know how long the airport will operate for, or how many planes will land on the runway
> 4 A reduction in the value of an asset, charged against profit (every year)

Notes

It is in fact only shares in *listed* companies that are easy to value, as they have a quoted share price. Valuing unlisted companies is much more difficult.

As mentioned in the subsequent section on Cash flow statements, *depreciation is* generally used for the loss of value of *tangible* assets (property, plant and equipment), and *amortization* for the loss of value of *intangible* assets (such as people, reputation, patents, trademarks, etc.).

Discussion

- It would be possible to put a value on a university's land and buildings, though this would not normally be done if the institution is a 'going concern' and consequently not for sale. Some old universities also have huge endowments, and large investment portfolios or sums of cash in the bank, which are easy to value, but famous universities are largely famous for the quality of their teaching and research staff.
- As with a university, if a company is a going concern and not for sale, the current selling price of its assets, or their replacement cost, is not relevant. Recording their historical cost is simpler and more objective. In many countries, a company's buildings can be depreciated down to €1 or whatever on the balance sheet, so no realistic figure is recorded anywhere. In countries with very high inflation, however, current or replacement cost accounting probably gives a better picture of a business's value.
- Accounting normally follows the principle of conservatism: one understates rather than overstates values or profits. Consequently raw materials, work-in-progress, and inventories are often recorded at 'the lower of cost or value', i.e. whichever figure is lower, the cost price or the current market value.
- Examples of companies whose value is largely based on brands or reputation include Coca-Cola, number one in Interbrand's ranking of the best global brands, with an estimated value of $66,667 billon in 2008 (http://www.interbrand.com). Similarly, Microsoft's value is far greater than its tangible assets.

Reading 2: Google Inc. Income statement

> **ANSWERS**
>
> 1 Interest Income Net
> 2 Research & Development
> 3 Cost of Revenue
> 4 Selling/General/Administrative Expenses

Vocabulary note

Google's Income statement has 'Net Income' (before and after tax), which is standard AmE. British companies usually use 'Profit'. Interestingly, the Swiss bank UBS publishes its annual reports and statements in English, but uses 'Net Profit', which is neither BrE nor AmE but perhaps an example of 'international English'.

Vocabulary: Cash flow statement

This exercise both introduces and recycles vocabulary and requires the learners to decide which of the three categories different items belong to.

Finance

ANSWERS

	Ops.	Inv.	Fin.
Amortization (loss of value of intangible assets)	✓		
Changes in the size of the inventory	✓		
Depreciation (loss of value of tangible assets)	✓		
Dividends paid			✓
Income taxes paid	✓		
Payments to suppliers for goods and services	✓		
Payments to employees	✓		
Proceeds from issuing shares or debt			✓
Purchases or sales of property, plant and equipment		✓	
Receipts from the sale of goods or services	✓		
Repurchase of company shares or repayment of debt			✓

Role play: Presenting a company's results

This role play will work best with learners who already know more about financial statements than is explained in this unit. To be interesting, it will need to be prepared out of class: explaining which figures have increased and which have decreased is straightforward; suggesting reasons as to *why* this happened will require research.

You could either select one learner from each group to make a presentation, or they could do whole group presentations (the CFO and colleagues).

In-service learners may prefer to talk about their own employer.

20 Market structure and competition

This unit begins with activities that practise the basic vocabulary of competitive markets, and continues with listening exercises based on an interview with a company director who talks about how new companies can change established industries or initiate new ones, and about how successful companies sometimes cluster together in the same geographical region. The unit ends with a case study concerning the development of an industrial cluster.

Lead-in

The questions here introduce the basic vocabulary. Learners are likely to know the names of some famous market leaders (e.g. Coca-Cola, Gillette, Ikea, Kellogg's, McDonald's, Nike, Nokia), and some, though probably fewer, market challengers (e.g. Pepsi, Burger King, Adidas). In other industries – such as automobiles, consumer electronics, white goods (fridges and cookers), cameras, and so on – they will probably know that there are several major manufacturers, without knowing which has the largest market share.

They will almost certainly also be able to give examples of products manufactured by market followers that they have bought, either because they were cheaper, or because they wanted something specialized.

Reading: Market structure

The Avis slogan referred to in the text was subsequently shortened to just 'We try harder.'

> **ANSWERS**
>
> **1** market leader **2** market share **3** market challenger **4** market followers **5** market segmentation **6** niche **7** differentiated **8** unique selling proposition

Vocabulary

This exercise defines words that appear in the subsequent listening activities.

> **ANSWERS**
>
> **1** cluster **2** landlord **3** entrepreneur **4** headhunter **5** attorney **6** vulnerable **7** patent **8** dominate **9** disrupt **10** address or tackle

Listening 1: Early stage companies
▶ 2.6

In answer to the pre-listening question, Charles Cotton mentions Cisco (who make networking components), eBay and Google. In the following extract he mentions Facebook.

> **AUDIO SCRIPT**
>
> **CHARLES COTTON** It's interesting to look at almost any industry from the perspective of an early stage company, and early stage companies get into an industry because they look at its structure and say, 'We can bring something to this industry which can potentially be highly disruptive and therefore change the landscape and give us as a company an opportunity to become fabulously successful,' and clearly there are examples of companies who've done that: Cisco going back 20 years had that sort of perspective, more recently companies like eBay invented a whole new approach, a whole new paradigm, and most recently of all you've got Google, that, you know, has evolved from a search company to compete with, you know, the biggest software companies on the planet, including the Microsofts who are now, you know, very concerned about that. So looking at all of these industries, some of them are defined by the new entrants, and I think eBay and Google are good examples of that, to an extent Cisco as well.

> **ANSWERS**
>
> **1** He says they think they can bring something new to an industry which can disrupt it and potentially make them extremely successful.
> **2** Cisco, eBay, Google and Microsoft

Finance

> **3** He means that the early companies in the industries come to dominate them (become the market leaders).

Note

Charles Cotton talks about 'the Microsofts', and in the next extract 'the Googles of this world'. This is a common expression used for giving an example of a certain category. It was also used by Chris Smart in **Unit 15**: in **Listening 4** he talked about 'the Ciscos of the world' and 'the Skypes of the world'.

Listening 2: Sine waves and bell curves ▶ 2.7

AUDIO SCRIPT

CHARLES COTTON And even now, Google is losing people, because Google has got itself into the situation where it's no longer that brash, young, successful, sexy start-up, and it's people like Facebook and so on who are now attracting the youngest and brightest away from the Googles of this world, and attracted to something yet again new, which again is disrupting the way in which, particularly young people communicate and converse with each other.

I think that we go through sort of sine waves or bell curves in industry where, you know, a disrupter moves in to being a dominant player, potentially with other strong players, but over time their position is, becomes more vulnerable, and they are, they find themselves being competed against by younger, newer, fresher, more exciting new ideas.

So, entrepreneurs, new ideas, disrupt, address, tackle, compete with existing, well-established industries and structures, but it's an evolution.

> **ANSWERS**
>
> - A sine wave has regular deviations from a horizontal axis over time, going from alternate highs to lows; a bell curve (showing a normal distribution of a quantitative phenomenon) rises and falls symmetrically around a vertical axis, giving approximately the shape of a bell. A bell curve is an image of the rise and fall of a particular company in an industry over time; a sine wave could illustrate the successive rise and fall of different companies. Business students, who have to devote much (if not most) of their time to maths and statistics, can be expected to know these concepts.
> - **1** The most intelligent young people in the computer industry now wanted to work for Facebook rather than Google
> - **2** **1** disrupter   **2** dominant   **3** vulnerable
>   **4** competed against   **5** entrepreneurs
>   **6** disrupt   **7** compete with
>   **8** well-established   **9** evolution

Discussion: Clusters

The concept of industrial or economic clusters was popularized by Michael Porter's well-known book *The Competitive Advantage of Nations* (New York: Free Press, 1990).

> **ANSWERS**
>
> - Bangalore: software developers
>   Detroit: automobiles   Hollywood: movies
>   Las Vegas: gambling (casinos)   Paris: fashion (haute couture)   Silicon Valley: computer companies   the area around Bordeaux: wine
> - There are many other industrial clusters that are less well-known internationally, but which may be known to learners from particular areas.
> - Start-ups situate themselves near other companies in the same industry because this helps them to find qualified staff, who might join them from other companies, and to have the possibility of exchanging information with other companies, and to benefit from the existence of ancillary service companies.

Market structure and competition **Unit 20**

- Similar shops and restaurants often situate themselves right next to each other because they know that this will attract a pool of potential customers, and they will probably get more custom this way than by choosing a location away from other similar businesses.

Listening 3: Clustering ▶2.8

AUDIO SCRIPT

CHARLES COTTON Clustering is perhaps the, one of the most exciting areas for governments as well as for companies to address. And everybody looks at the well-established examples. In America, it used to be around one, Route 128, around Boston area which really lost its crown to Silicon Valley, out in northern California. And today there are many examples of clusters. Each of these clusters has a number of factors associated with them, no one of which is sufficient on its own to define a cluster, but these factors in total, perhaps eight out of ten of them, you know, are to be found in every cluster. If you look at the traditional ones like Route 128, like Silicon Valley, and in Europe places like Tel Aviv, like Cambridge, like Oxford, like London, they've all evolved around a university campus, and what you've got there then are very bright people pushing the boundaries of science and technology, and seeing then the opportunities for the development of companies, and for those companies then to be successful.

What happens as a result of that is that people move from a university environment into a, into a business environment and need to learn new skills, and so what you have around those people that make that step are people, older people who've been in industry before, or people who are focusing on supporting products and services and so on, and you get this sort of virtuous circle taking place where you have a nucleus which is the individual or individuals who break away from university, then massing up as they talk to each other to gain experience, talk to other people to gain experience, and build around them this, this cluster.

So some of the other factors that make clusters successful are all of the supporting services like the lawyers, the accountants, the patent attorneys, the headhunters, the recruiters, the people who provide catering services for the companies that come along, the landlords and so on, so you get this vast circle of activity around, around a cluster, which then builds into something more than what starts as a technology cluster into a, into an economic cluster itself ...

ANSWERS

1 Route 128 around Boston and Silicon Valley in northern California
2 Tel Aviv, Cambridge, Oxford and London
3 The existence of a very good university, with science and technology departments
4 They need to learn new business and management skills
5 1 patent attorneys   2 headhunters
   3 landlords   4 technology   5 economic

Note

Some people may object to Charles Cotton's situating of Tel Aviv in Europe, but he is speaking loosely, as when he speaks of Czechoslovakia (which has not existed as such since the end of 1992) in the following section.

Listening 4: Software-based clusters ▶2.9

If you consider that there is too much listening and not enough reading in this unit, you could of course replace some of these listening exercises, e.g. this one and/or the following one, by reading activities, given that the audio scripts are included in the Student's Book.

- Many learners may offer India as an answer to the pre-listening question, but in fact Charles Cotton is talking about eastern Europe.

Finance

AUDIO SCRIPT

CHARLES COTTON ... so it becomes a question of saying, well, what is it about your culture, the background, the technologies, the history of your industries that can provide the essence of what your cluster can be grouped around? You may not have a world-class university which these other ones have, but you may have some fabulous software programmers, and certainly if you look at places in eastern Europe and Russia, because they couldn't afford the latest computers and so on back in the 90s, and two, and sort of, you know, the 1980s and 1990s, their software programmers were outstanding, they were the most creative people on the planet, and they've continued to evolve in that way and today it's certainly the case that software developers in Bulgaria, in Hungary, in Czechoslovakia, in parts of Ukraine and so on, are in great demand for two reasons. First of all, they have this ability to do a great deal with very small levels of resource, and secondly they don't charge as much as programmers in the western world or even India these days, because India started as sort of a crèche, almost, of software developers, but has now become a much more expensive place to have that software done, so there are always opportunities creating, and around, being created, and around those opportunities can coalesce many of the other factors that can lead to a cluster formation, and so today I'm most particularly aware of the software-based clusters for development purposes in eastern Europe and the former parts of the Soviet Union.

ANSWERS

1 Software programmers in eastern Europe (Bulgaria, Hungary, 'Czechoslovakia' and parts of Ukraine) and Russia
2 Because they didn't have the latest computers in the 1980s and 1990s, so they developed the ability to do a great deal with very limited resources
3 They are much cheaper than Indian programmers (they don't charge as much)

Listening 5: Clusters of the future
▶ 2.10

AUDIO SCRIPT

CHARLES COTTON But as we look forward I think we're going to see, you know, new powerhouses economically evolve, which will inevitably mean that there will be new clusters created. The ones that most people tend to talk around are round China and India, but I also propose that we'll see similar things happening in places like Brazil, and Brazil is a resource-rich country with, you know, an increasingly well-educated population, and I think education is at the core of any of these clusters, which is why China and India are going to become so successful, because particularly in their cases, a lot of their young people have gone off to be educated in, principally in the US but also in Europe, and then have gone back because they've seen the business opportunities in their own country. In a way we're going to see similar sorts of things happening with, with places like Brazil which has got a very large population, which is resource-rich as I mentioned, and where a lot of the population has experience of being in university in North America, and again seeing opportunities in their homeland to create something special, and along the way, you know, being a capitalist-dominated world, you know, seeing the opportunity for personal gain for, you know, the exercise of their knowledge and their skills.

ANSWERS

1 China, India and Brazil
2 They have increasingly well-educated populations: people who have gone to university in the US and Europe, and returned to their country because they see business opportunities

• Learners may suggest other European, Asian or Latin American countries that could successfully develop economic clusters. Africa seems to be less likely, as does Australia for anything that has to be exported.

Case study: Encouraging clusters

This is a fairly abstract case study, given that no countries or industries are specified, but learners should be able to say whether at least some of these factors are present in their country (e.g. a skilled workforce, a good infrastructure, a good education system, already-existing companies). They may know less about the actual business environment, government services, the existence or otherwise of venture capital firms, and the ease of mobility.

You could also attempt to elicit the factors listed here with the students' books closed, before beginning the case study.

The learners may have discussed the different sectors and industries in their country, and their possible evolution, in **Unit 7**.

All countries should have at least one sector or industry that already has or could potentially develop a competitive advantage, and which could usefully be backed by the government. Some minor form of government help is clearly a more plausible prescription than 'develop a world-class university', or 'establish an excellent infrastructure'.

Depending on time (and perhaps on how different their recommendations are), one, two or all of the groups could present their conclusions to the class.

Writing

This could be written either individually or in groups. The groups' conclusions and recommendations could conceivably be changed by input from the rest of the class, following the presentations.

21 Takeovers

This unit contains a text about takeovers, mergers and leveraged buyouts and accompanying exercises, extracts from an interview with the Press Officer of the UK Competition Commission, and a role play about a potential investigation of a large and successful company by a competition authority.

Lead-in

The first three questions are answered in the text which follows. If the learners know about the subject, you could add further questions, and try to elicit the information contained in the text.

Reading: Takeovers, mergers and buyouts

The text is quite dense, as it defines all the terms included in the Vocabulary exercise which follows; learners who are not familiar with the subject may well need to read it at least twice.

> **SUGGESTED ANSWERS**
>
> The following sentences should probably be underlined:
> - Why do companies take over other companies?
>   Successful companies have to find ways of using their profits.
>   ... sometimes it is easier to take over other companies with existing products and customers.
>   Acquiring a competitor in the same field of activity (horizontal integration) gives a company a larger market share and reduces competition.
>   Companies can also acquire businesses involved in other parts of their supply chain (vertical integration), generally to achieve cost savings.
> - How do companies take over other companies?
>   ... a raid, which simply involves buying as many of a company's stocks as possible on the stock market.
>   ... a takeover bid: a public offer to a company's stockholders to buy their stocks at a certain price (above the current market price) during a limited period of time.
> - What is a merger?
>   ... to merge with it: to combine the two companies to form a single new one.

Note

The book mentioned in the final paragraph is *Barbarians at the Gate: The Fall of RJR Nabisco*, by Bryan Burrough and John Helyar (New York: Harper and Row, 1990); 20th anniversary edition (New York: HarperBusiness, 2008).

Other examples of the bad reputation of corporate raiders in the 1980s are two well-known movies, Oliver Stone's *Wall Street* (1987), starring Michael Douglas as a raider whose mantra is 'Greed is good', and Garry Marshall's *Pretty Woman* (1990), with Richard Gere and Julia Roberts.

Vocabulary note

The noun *takeover* is one word but the verb *take over* is two. Although investment banks have Mergers and Acquisitions departments, most people (including financial journalists) talk about *takeovers* rather than *acquisitions*. In everyday language, the verb *buy* is much more common than *acquire* (or *purchase*).

The text uses the terms *stock* and *stockholder* (because there are more and bigger takeovers in the US than the UK); the British equivalents *share* and *shareholder* have the same meanings.

Vocabulary

> **ANSWERS**
>
> **1** diversify   **2** retail outlets   **3** controlling interest   **4** listed companies   **5** fees   **6** conglomerates   **7** synergy   **8** market capitalization   **9** subsidiaries   **10** pension fund

Comprehension

> **SUGGESTED ANSWERS**
>
> 1 Horizontal integration means buying competitors in the same field of activity; vertical integration means buying companies involved in other parts of the supply chain.
> 2 Backward integration means buying suppliers of raw materials or components; forward integration means buying distributors or retailers.
> 3 A raid means buying a company's stocks on the stock market; a takeover bid means making an offer to a company's stockholders to buy their stocks.
> 4 A friendly bid is when the directors of a company agree to a takeover; a hostile bid is when they do not.
> 5 Asset-stripping means buying a company in order to sell its profitable parts, or to close the company and sell its assets at a profit.

Discussion

Business learners may well have read or been told that the possibility of a takeover is a challenge to company managers and directors to do their jobs well, and to put capital to productive use. If they fail to do this, they will be taken over by companies or raiders who will use the assets more efficiently, cut costs, and increase shareholder value. On the other hand, the permanent threat of a takeover or a buyout is clearly a disincentive to long-term planning or capital investment, as a company will lose its investment if a raider tries to break it up if its share price disappoints in the short term. Takeovers can also lead to job losses, which is the subject of **Unit 25, Efficiency and employment**.

Listening 1: The role of the Competition Commission ▶ 2.11

Rory Taylor speaks rather quickly; learners may need to listen two or three times in order to fully understand, and answer the questions.

AUDIO SCRIPT

RORY TAYLOR We're a competition investigation authority; it's what the Americans might call an antitrust authority. Our role is, when cases are referred to us, to look at mergers that might have the effect of damaging competition in a particular market, or indeed in certain cases we can look at the markets in general, and again see whether competition is working effectively, and benefiting the consumer.

We do have a free market attitude in this country, but markets left unchecked can develop features that are damaging to competition and, by definition, towards consumers. If you can imagine a situation, hypothetically, in which one company just became more and more successful there would be the danger that they could just buy over every single other company in that market, and ultimately that wouldn't be good for anyone in the economy, including the company itself.

We always say round here that good, efficient companies have nothing to fear from the competition authorities, and we've had plenty of companies come through here and tell us that competition is essential to keeping their business efficient and innovative, so it's, it's an essential part of the system, and I think if you look at any developed economy there's, there's always a competition regime there. How it works differs from country to country, but I think there's a general acceptance that it's a necessary, a necessary check and balance as long as it's not over-interventionist.

> **ANSWERS**
>
> 1 An antitrust authority (A trust means a group or consortium of independent organizations formed in order to limit competition by controlling the production and distribution of a product or service, but antitrust laws are also applied to single large companies that dominate a market.)
> 2 If a proposed merger might damage competition in a particular market, or if it is thought that competition is not working effectively, and benefiting the consumer, in a particular market. (This could also apply to proposed takeovers.)

Finance

3 A company that is so successful that it could buy every single other company in its market. (Rory Taylor says 'buy over'; 'buy up' or just 'buy' would be more common.)
4 That having competition (rival, competing companies) is essential to keeping their business efficient and innovative
5 a A belief that markets should be allowed to operate without governmental interference
   b A set of laws and regulations concerning markets and competition
   c A way of preventing abuse of power by strong companies. (The term comes from theories of government, particularly political systems which have legislative, executive, and judicial branches, each with separate powers, as in the USA.)
   d Intervening or interfering too much in what is supposed to be a free market

Listening 2: Market investigations ▶ 2.12

AUDIO SCRIPT

RORY TAYLOR You won't generally come across too many markets where there's one dominant player outside the, sort of, natural monopolies and the utilities. We used to do, under the previous legislation, what were called monopoly investigations, but now they're known as market investigations, as to some extent that reflects that you're not usually looking at one player dominating one particular market but maybe a small handful. That's not necessarily a bad thing, it all depends on the structure of that market and to what degree they're competing with each other. We've just been looking at the groceries market, that's … I would say using, using the term advisedly, dominated by big four supermarkets, certainly got the lion's share of the … people's shopping, but at the same time they're competing very vigorously with each other, so that's not necessarily anything we'd, we'd look to intervene in.

For questions 2 and 3, learners could work in pairs to deduce meanings, and consult dictionaries if necessary.

ANSWERS

1 **1** player **2** natural monopolies **3** utilities **4** market investigations **5** handful **6** groceries **7** lion's share

2 **1** company or competitor or business **5** (a small) number or quantity **7** the largest part

3 **2** A market in which it is normal that there is only one company (a monopoly) as it would be difficult, or impossible, or uneconomic to provide competing services (e.g. water or gas pipes, electric cables, etc.)
3 Service providers such as water, electricity and gas companies
6 Food and other everyday products bought in supermarkets

Listening 3: Breaking the law and abusing a dominant position ▶ 2.13

AUDIO SCRIPT

RORY TAYLOR We look at the structure of markets and whether markets are working competitively. Now even if they're not working competitively that can be a range of factors that doesn't mean the company is doing anything wrong, it just means they're acting logically, to whatever business and competitive pressures there are. On the other side of the coin, there are offences, breaches of competition law. Those actually get looked at by the Office of Fair Trading, and that's where companies have actively, are actively, in simple terms, doing something wrong. There's two offences. One is abuse of a dominant position. The, probably the highest-profile example of that in recent times is the Microsoft case, with the European Competition Commission, and the other one is cartels, or price fixing as it's also known, which is something that our sister body the Office of Fair Trading are being, are taking a great interest at the moment, and yeah, that is something that's looked [at] extremely seriously by the authorities and you can be fined as much as 10% of your annual turnover, so you can be facing big fines if you are, if you are found guilty of that thing.

ANSWERS

1 a, b, d
2 The European Competition Commission and the Office of Fair Trading
3 Price-fixing, or forming a cartel (a group of companies which agree not to compete on price)

Note

Regarding question 1b, *holding* a dominant position is not against the law, only *abusing* such a position; as Taylor puts it, 'it doesn't mean the company is doing anything wrong, it just means they're acting logically, to whatever business and competitive pressures there are.'

Discussion

- Abusing a dominant position means using your huge market share (or near monopoly) to:
  - charge low prices (below the cost of production) in order to drive a competitor out of business ('predatory pricing')
  - impose unfair purchase or selling prices or other unfair trading conditions (such as supplementary obligations on suppliers)
  - limit production, markets or technical development to the prejudice of consumers, in order to keep prices high
  - apply different conditions to equivalent transactions with other trading parties
  - refuse to sell individual products, but only more expensive 'bundled' products (sometimes called 'tied selling'), etc.
- The Microsoft case was about the company, which had a near monopoly with its operating system, only selling it combined with additional programs such as a web browser and a media player, which prevented other companies competing against these products.

Other cases that have been investigated by US and European regulators include telecoms companies, airlines, microchip producers, supermarkets, oil companies, etc. A web search for 'antitrust cases' will give numerous examples.

Role play: Is this company restricting competition?

There are three role cards at the back of the Student's Book on pages 146, 148 and 150. If the learners are unable to choose an industry to which their imaginary dominant company belongs, you will have to choose for them.

There is an imbalance among the roles, as the company has two representatives to the competition authority's one. This is because the company has rather more arguments than the competition authority, at least as shown on the role cards. This imbalance could be corrected by giving the competition authority's investigator a colleague or assistant, but the role cards will still give more arguments to the company!

Once the class has chosen an industry, the learners can either do the role play in groups of three, or prepare the roles in pairs or small groups first.

Writing

No model answer is given here, as the summary is likely to contain many words and phrases, if not sentences, from the role cards at the back of the Student's Book.

See the role plays 'Who should we take over?' and 'Integration' in *Business Roles* by John Crowther-Alwyn (Cambridge University Press).

22 Government and taxation

This is the first of seven units on economics. The role of the government has been a major political and economic issue in industrialized democracies since at least the 1980s. Although the number of nationalized (government-owned) industries is steadily declining in most parts of the world, people with left-wing views still generally believe that the government has an essential role to play in ensuring the provision of services such as education, healthcare, social security, public transport and perhaps housing, and regulating working conditions, health and safety standards, and so on. People with right-wing views, on the contrary, generally argue that many (or most, or maybe all) of these activities can be left to private enterprise and the market system, and that the role of the government should be restricted to activities such as defence, the police, and the justice system. They argue that too much regulation is bad for business, and leads to inefficiency, and therefore unemployment. This is an argument that is *not* going to go away.

This unit has discussion activities about the role of government and the pros and cons of taxation, an extract from a famously anti-government book by Milton Friedman, and the first of four listening exercises based on extracts from an interview with Michael Kitson, a Cambridge economist. In this one, he outlines what he considers to be necessary government interventions in the economy.

Lead-in

As usual, there are no 'right answers' here. Learners in comparatively inexpensive public universities can generally see the advantages of government spending. Few of them are likely to believe that the armed services or the police and the justice system should be privatized, although there are private prisons in some countries (such as the USA). Many of them can be expected to approve of a mixed system of both public and private education and healthcare, and the provision of some low-income housing. Some countries have privatized public transport systems, with varying results. There have long been proponents of privatizing social security, though one hears less from them during financial crises and stock market crashes. When asked to think about it, most business students seem to see the utility of regulated working conditions, traffic regulations, health and safety legislation, and so on. Similarly, few people believe in the totally unregulated sale of alcohol, drugs, guns, and so on.

Reading: The role of government

These extracts are from Chapter Two, 'The Tyranny of Controls', of *Free to Choose* (London: Penguin, 1980), pp. 88–94, by Milton Friedman and his wife Rose.

BACKGROUND NOTES

Milton Friedman (1912–2006) was a leading 'Chicago School' free market economist, and an opponent of Keynesianism. He was a monetarist who stressed the importance of the quantity of money as an instrument of government policy and as a determinant of business cycles and inflation. He described himself as a classical liberal and a libertarian, and was an opponent of much government regulation, and a staunch defender of individual freedom. Many of his policy prescriptions can safely be described as highly controversial, but his ideas on privatization and deregulation were taken up in the 1980s by the Reagan administration in the US, and the Thatcher government in the UK, and were later influential in many central and eastern European countries. Friedman won the Nobel Prize for Economics in 1976.

Vocabulary notes

Liberal is a very problematic word, which means different things to different people. For *Americans,* a liberal is someone who believes in state intervention in the economy, such as Democrat presidents like Kennedy, Clinton and Obama. The opposite, which applies to recent Republican presidents, is *conservative.*

But in *Britain,* the Liberals (now the Liberal Democrats) were for many years the centre party, between Labour (socialist or social democrat) and the Conservatives. Consequently in Britain, a liberal is someone who is neither on the left nor right.

Yet in pure economic terms, dating from the early 19th century, *liberal* denotes a belief in free markets, without governmental intervention, and is thus part of the name of right-wing political parties in many European countries and languages, for whom Milton Friedman would be an excellent example of a liberal, or what today is often called a neo-liberal.

> **ANSWER**
>
> In the Friedmans' opinion, the role of the US government has expanded far too much. Its interventions in the economy might even end economic progress. The government severely limits people's freedom to spend their money and work as they choose. There is a need to end a lot of existing restrictions.

Comprehension

> **ANSWERS**
>
> 1 They believe that government intervention – limitations imposed on economic freedom – threatens to end 200 years of economic progress.
> 2 'Currently, more than 40% of our income is disposed of on our behalf by government at federal, state and local levels combined.'
> 3 They disapprove of laws that prevent physicians (doctors) prescribing some drugs (medicines) that have been banned in the US, and that make it compulsory to have seat belts in cars.
> 4 All business activities and transactions should be voluntary, and nobody should use force or coercion.
> 5 They believe that workers should be free to work any number of hours they agree with their employer, without restrictions imposed by the government.

Vocabulary notes

The Friedman text uses the American words *automobile* and *railroad*; the British say *car* and *railway*. Similarly, Americans use *truck* and *airplane*, while the British say *lorry* and *aeroplane*. As mentioned in the Student's Book,

Americans say *physician* where the British usually say *doctor*. They also say *mortician* (a person who prepares the dead for burial or cremation, and arranges funerals) while the British say *undertaker*. But, of course, the verb *to undertake* means to do or to promise to do something; undertaker is *not* another word for entrepreneur.

Discussion

As mentioned above, the Friedmans are best described as classical liberals and libertarians, although in US terms they are also clearly arch conservatives.

Learners may agree with some of their arguments, though many will be shocked by the implication that *anyone* should be able to practise as a lawyer, a physician, a dentist, etc. without some kind of government certification (a permit or a licence). (The Friedmans' argument is that 'the market' would decide and bad lawyers, doctors and dentists would go out of business, and that it is part of one's individual responsibility to find out if a lawyer or doctor or dentist is any good.)

Vocabulary

> **ANSWERS**
>
> 1 B   2 G   3 D   4 A   5 E   6 F   7 C

If the learners find this exercise difficult, you could suggest that they use dictionaries, working in pairs.

Listening: Government intervention
▶ 2.14

> **AUDIO SCRIPT**
>
> **MICHAEL KITSON** … The second effect is whether we think unfettered free markets alone can ensure the long-term optimal allocation of resources and long-term economic growth. Markets are very important, I'm not denying that, but so is the role of government to actually help markets work better. Often economists talk

about notions of market failure or the fact that markets are not working properly.

Let's just think of some of the areas where governments should want to intervene. They may want to spend, spend money on education, it's very important, educated workforce. People may not invest enough in their education if they have to pay for it themselves, and many people wouldn't be able to access the resources, wouldn't be able to get the credit, OK, so it's the importance of education. Similar things apply to health, we may not actually buy enough health if we are left to buy it ourselves.

Let's think about developing new products and technologies. Developing new products and technologies is highly risky and highly expensive, and highly uncertain outcomes, but possibly very big outcomes for the economy as a whole. So it makes … it's understandable that firms do not invest in very early-stage technologies, OK, and … because it may be very expensive for them, there's a good chance they won't succeed, and if they do succeed, somebody else will be able to copy and replicate and benefit from their effects.

These are positive externality effects of government intervention. If government helps to commercialize science, develop new ideas, those products can then at a later stage be developed and employed by the market, and by businesses.

I think there are many areas. This is about government in terms of economic growth. I think it's mainly in terms of the areas of education, particularly, again in the areas of transport and networks and infrastructure, and increasingly in helping develop science, and helping commercialize science, and bringing those ideas, which you know, ideas ultimately drive long-term economic growth, and encouraging those ideas from a science base to become new products, new services, better ways of doing things, will make economic growth happen in the future.

ANSWERS

- Kitson is clearly in favour of some government interventions in the economy.

1 1 free markets   2 optimal   3 economic growth   4 market failure

2 An educated workforce is important, and people may not spend or invest enough in their education or health if they have to pay for it themselves, or be able to get the credit (borrow money) to do so

3 Because it's highly risky and highly expensive, and has highly uncertain outcomes, and because other companies might copy or replicate and benefit from the technology they develop

4 Transport and networks and infrastructure, and developing and helping commercialize science

Learners do not have to agree with Kitson about these various forms of spending, but many can be expected to.

Note

This extract begins with 'The second effect …'; Kitson had previously mentioned what he calls the first effect of government intervention, which is trying to counteract the business cycle. This part of the interview is in the Listening section of **Unit 23**.

Discussion: Taxation 1

- Learners may not know the English names for the usual taxes (which are included in the following Vocabulary exercise), but they will probably know the concepts. For example, in most countries:
  - consumers pay sales tax or value-added tax on most products sold in shops and stores
  - most people pay income tax on their wages or salary (unless this is extremely low)
  - inheritances are usually subject to an inheritance tax
  - gains from shares and other securities are often liable to capital gains tax
  - most countries have customs duties on imports, either from all foreign countries, or from those not part of a customs union such as the EU or NAFTA
  - other common taxes include excise duties on petrol, tobacco and alcohol, road tax on cars, and stamp duty on property and financial transactions.

- Examples of the same amount of money being taxed more than once include business profits – companies pay tax on their profits and shareholders pay income tax on dividends – and individual wealth, which is usually taxed (income tax, capital gains tax, inheritance tax) when it is first received but in some countries is taxed again annually (usually at a low rate) by a wealth tax if it is not spent, and is subject to sales taxes if it is spent.

BACKGROUND INFORMATION

Benjamin Franklin (1706–90) was an American statesman (he helped write the Declaration of Independence) and a scientist (he invented the lightning conductor). His line about death and taxes is still widely quoted. He is not necessarily one of the people in the cartoon!

Vocabulary

ANSWERS

1 B 2 A 3 B 4 B 5 C 6 A 7 B 8 C
9 C 10 B 11 C 12 C

Notes

In several European languages, the equivalent term for *tax haven* uses a translation of the word *paradise*, a synonym for *heaven* (e.g. *Steuerparadies, paradis fiscal, paradiso fiscale*, etc.). But *haven* means harbour (*Hafen* in German, *havre* in French).

Loophole is of course pronounced loop-hole, not loofole.

Discussion: Taxation 2

ANSWERS

There are no 'correct answers' to questions 1, 2, 3 and 5. Wealth taxes only exist in a few countries (such as Germany and Switzerland). Many people approve of progressive tax rates until they get rich! The main reason for having both direct and indirect taxes is that indirect taxes when you go shopping are less *visible* than, say, 40% immediately deducted from your salary.

4 Speech bubbles 1, 3, 6, 7, 10, 12 and 13 are clearly in favour of taxation and government spending (on the transport infrastructure, education, health, welfare, the urban environment, etc.). Speech bubbles 2, 4, 5, 8, 9 and 11 are clearly against taxation.

Presentation: Taxation and government spending

This could be prepared in pairs or small groups. Even learners without opinions of their own should be able to construct a short talk or written report from the material in this unit. Given that there are arguments on both sides, this would be an opportunity to use various connectors and conjunctions such as:

e.g. (for example)	for instance	similarly	
therefore	consequently	as a result	so
because	since	as	
because of	due to	owing to (+ noun phrase)	
in order to	so as to		
though	although	even though	
however	yet	nevertheless	nonetheless
while	whereas		
what's more	furthermore	moreover	in addition
on the other hand	on the contrary	alternatively	
i.e. (that is)	in other words		

23 The business cycle

This unit is about the business cycle, its causes, and whether governments can do anything to change it. There are (unusually) two reading texts, with accompanying vocabulary and comprehension exercises, and a second extract from the interview with Michael Kitson.

Lead-in

This book is being written during a huge international financial crisis, often referred to as the 'credit crunch' (see Units 14 and 16). There is no question that the global economy is currently doing badly: see, for example, the British GDP graph in the Student's Book. What will happen next is unknown, but recessions generally end after 18 months or so.

The main causes of the alternate periods of growth and contraction (or what economists like to call 'negative growth') of the business cycle are discussed in this unit. The most important one seems to be the level of consumption: the decisions of millions of people whether to spend their money and borrow more, when the economic outlook is good, or spend less and save more, when the economic outlook is bad or when interest rates rise.

Vocabulary 1: The business cycle

> **ANSWERS**
>
> 1 downturn   2 upturn   3 expectations
> 4 consumption   5 balance of payments
> 6 gross domestic product (GDP)   7 demand
> 8 supply   9 save

Note
Economists also talk about gross national product (GNP), which is GDP plus income from overseas investments minus the earnings of foreign investors in the home economy.

Reading 1: What causes the business cycle?

Before reading this text you could ask questions about the GDP graph (When were there big recessions? When was there a long upturn? etc.). Or ask the learners to describe the graph, if they are likely to know verbs like:

> remain stable, stabilize, level off, rise, increase, grow, peak, reach a peak, fall, decrease, decline, bottom out, etc.

and adjectives and adverbs of size or quantity such as:

> slight/slightly, dramatic/dramatically, considerable/considerably, sharp/sharply, significant/significantly, substantial/substantially

and adjectives and adverbs of time such as:

> gradual/gradually, slow/slowly, steady/steadily, sudden/suddenly, rapid/rapidly.

> **ANSWERS**
>
> 1 gross domestic product (GDP)   2 upturn
> 3 downturn   4 consumption   5 expectations
> 6 balance of payments   7 save   8 demand
> 9 supply

Comprehension

> **SUGGESTED ANSWERS**
>
> 1 ... the demand for goods and services declines.
> 2 ... economic times are good and they feel confident about the future.
> 3 ... they are afraid of losing their jobs / becoming unemployed.
> 4 ... people have to pay more on their mortgage or rent (and so consume less).
> 5 ... consumption is increasing.
> 6 ... innovations destroy established companies or industries.

Discussion

- An obvious example of 'creative destruction' currently occurring is the way free news on the Internet threatens traditional newspapers, and possibilities to download music and films threaten the 'old-fashioned' CD and DVD industry. Similarly free internet telephone services such as Skype threaten 'traditional' telecommunications companies.
- Whether the government should intervene in the economy, by creating demand or jobs during a recession, divides the political left and right, and Keynesian and free market economists. The Keynesian argument (named after the English economist John Maynard Keynes, whose famous book *The General Theory of Employment, Interest and Money* was published in 1936), is that governments can increase demand and employment by way of fiscal or monetary policy, either by public works (building roads, schools, etc.), or by decreasing taxes, lowering interest rates, or increasing the money supply, so that consumers have more money to spend. The argument in favour of public works is that it makes more sense to pay people to create something than to pay them unemployment benefits to do nothing. Arguments against this include the one that government spending 'crowds out' or reduces the amount of money or credit available to private companies, thereby hindering the revival of the economy.

    Although governments can still make tax and spending decisions, in many countries they no longer have control over interest rate decisions (concerning the base rate – the rate at which the central bank lends money to commercial banks, which influences all other rates) as the central bank is independent from the government. Similarly, decisions about the money supply – the amount of money available in the economy – are now often made by the central bank rather than the government. The most common way of changing the money supply is by selling short-term bonds, called treasury bills, to commercial banks (to take money out of circulation), or buying them back (to increase the amount of money in circulation).

- The arguments against such governmental spending are outlined in the second reading text. Monetarists argue that increasing the money supply when the same amount of goods and services are available will simply raise prices and lead to inflation. Another argument is that fiscal measures usually only take effect too late, when the economy is already recovering, and therefore merely augment the next swing in the business cycle.

Vocabulary 2: Fiscal and monetary policy

ANSWERS

1 C   2 A   3 B   4 E   5 D   6 G   7 F

2 boost – stimulate   decrease – reduce
   depression – slump   excess – surplus
   expand – grow   expenditure – spending
   output – production   recovery – upturn

3 boom – depression   contract – expand
   demand – supply   endogenous – exogenous   peak – trough   save – spend

Pronunciation note

Learners unfamiliar with the word *trough* will probably not be able to guess its correct pronunciation (/trɒf/), given that there are at least nine different ways of pronouncing the letters *-ough* in English, as in *though, through, thought, thorough, trough, tough, bough, hiccough* and *lough* (the Irish version of the Scottish *loch* or lake).

Listening 1: Consumption and the business cycle ▶ 2.15

Note that Michael Kitson was speaking in early 2008.

AUDIO SCRIPT

MICHAEL KITSON   ... Perhaps a year ago that question would have been considered redundant by many economists. The business cycle has ended, we now have nice economic growth, you know, consistent economic growth and the business cycle has ended, and inflation's ended. Actually the reality is that inflation is still on the horizon, and the potential of a downturn in the economy. I tend to think about the major components of aggregate demand, and how that drives economic growth.

Booms [are] particularly driven by consumption, and consumption is particularly driven when people have positive expectations, their assets are increasing, particularly housing, encourages people to spend, OK. Depressions are actually that process goes into reverse, particularly when credit becomes no longer available, assets tend to decline in value, people tend to start saving more and consume less. I think consumption, particularly for the advanced countries, is the major driver of the business cycle, and the major driver of consumption is the availability of credit and the value of assets, of which houses are the most crucial one. So I tend to think it's very … people spending or not spending.

ANSWERS

1 That the business cycle and inflation had ended, and there was now consistent economic growth
2 No; he says there's still the potential of both inflation and a downturn in the economy
3 Increased spending and consumption when people have positive expectations, and when their assets, particularly the price of their house, are increasing
4 Depressions occur when people start saving more and consuming less, when credit is no longer available, and assets decline in value.

Listening 2: Keynesianism ▶ 2.16

BACKGROUND INFORMATION

John Maynard Keynes (1883–1946) (pronounced *canes* or /keɪnz/) was the most influential economist of the mid-20th century, to the extent that he has a school of economic thought named after him – and indeed has his name in an adjective and noun in many languages (Keynesian/Keynesianism, keynésien, keynesianische, keynesiano, etc.).

His ideas about government intervention in the economy, and the use of fiscal and monetary measures to diminish the effects of economic recessions and periods of high employment, were put into practice by many major Western economies shortly before the end of the Great Depression in the 1930s. Keynes argued against the traditional view that free markets would automatically provide full employment as long as workers reduced their wage demands. Keynesian economic policies were widely adopted in the 1950s and 60s. In 1971 the Republican US President Richard Nixon famously said 'We are all Keynesians now,' but by the end of the 1970s, the monetarist argument that Keynesian policies inevitably lead to inflation had become dominant. As mentioned in the following Reading text (and as most learners will know), Keynesianism made a dramatic return in the crisis of 2008.

Keynes was part of the British delegation at the Versailles Peace Conference after World War I, and in 1944 he was the leader of the British delegation at the Bretton Woods negotiations (see the Teacher's Book notes to Unit 26). Keynes was also part of the 'Bloomsbury Group' of writers and art critics and intellectuals, which included Virginia Woolf and E. M. Forster. He was also a very successful investor. At the time of his death his private fortune was worth about £500,000 (about £11 million in 2009 money). He also increased the value of King's College, Cambridge's portfolio from £30,000 to £380,000, during a period (1924–1946) when the British stock market fell by 15%. (By way of contrast, the neoclassical economist Irving Fisher, known for his quantity theory of money, infamously stated that 'Stock prices have reached what looks like a permanently high plateau,' and 'I expect to see the stock market a good deal higher within a few months' on 17 October 1929, a week before the great crash. Fisher was responsible for Yale University's endowment, which lost most of its value.)

AUDIO SCRIPT

MICHAEL KITSON   … we still have the business cycle, OK, we can still have the possible problems of a downturn, which makes the argument for what I think is standard Keynesianism, the way you manipulate budget balances or budget deficits depending on whether the economy's booming or is in recession. OK, and the government's golden rule in the UK is consistent with that, in general. If the economy's turning down it may make sense for governments to have budget deficits, and to keep expenditure in the economy. That's the Keynesianism argument about ironing out the business cycle, which I think is important because recessions can have very long-term harmful effects.

> **ANSWERS**
>
> 1 **1** downturn **2** manipulate **3** balances
>   **4** deficits **5** booming **6** recession
>   **7** expenditure **8** harmful
> 2 C
> 3 Here, ironing out means to try to flatten the business cycle, to make its upward and downward swings smaller. More generally, to iron out means to solve problems or find solutions.

Notes

The temptation for governments to cut taxes and increase spending in the months before an election (answer 2A), so as to temporarily increase people's disposable income and reduce unemployment, is precisely the reason why many countries (including the Euro-zone and Britain) now have central banks which are independent of the government.

Answer 2B (the government should ensure that there is never a budget deficit) might please monetarists and fiscal conservatives, but it is not the policy of most governments, which still believe in borrowing money and intervening in the economy when necessary.

Answer 2D (the government should spend any budget surplus on boosting or stimulating the economy) would be ridiculous; the other side of Keynesianism involves trying to slow down growth when the economy appears to be 'overheating' – when industry is working at full productive capacity, and consumption and investment are leading to inflation. Besides, virtually all countries have massive national debts that should ideally be repaid at some point.

Reading 2: Keynesianism and monetarism

> **ANSWERS**
>
> The paragraph headings come in this order:
> D C E A B

Comprehension

> **ANSWERS**
>
> **1** C **2** A **3** B **4** E **5** F **6** G **7** D

Discussion: Government intervention

There are, once again, no 'right answers' here. The first two questions echo the last two questions in the previous discussion activity. If it is accepted that increasing or inflating the money supply leads to price inflation, arguments for and against Keynesianism (or Keynesianism vs monetarism) come down to arguments in favour of either a stable price level (little or no inflation) or low unemployment.

Similarly, whether governments should rescue 'dinosaurs' in declining industries, or instead invest in start-ups in new industries, is a matter of opinion.

24 Corporate social responsibility

Some people argue that the objective of business, and consequently the role of managers, is to make as much money as possible for companies' owners, the stockholders or shareholders. Other people argue that companies have to be careful never to cheat customers, but for purely business reasons, rather than ethical ones: disappointed customers will not buy any more of your products in future. Still other people insist that companies have social and ethical responsibilities to their customers, their staff, their business partners, their local community, society in general, and the natural environment, that are as important as, or more important than, their responsibility to provide a financial return to their shareholders. This unit includes a text containing opposing views of the social responsibilities of business, listening exercises based on further extracts from the interview with Anna-Kim Hyun-Seung, discussion activities concerning the ethics of various business practices, and a role play about problems facing a clothing manufacturer.

Lead-in

A good way to introduce this topic, before even looking at the illustration, would be to refer to – or better still, elicit from the learners – recent news stories relating to ethical or unethical behaviour by well-known companies.

There are clearly no 'right answers' as to which of the views expressed in the illustration the learners should agree with, but here are some remarks.

The first view is somewhat discredited these days, although placing the person expressing it in front of a dozen smoking chimneys is perhaps unfair. The second view – *caveat emptor* – clearly contradicts modern marketing theory, and the logic of satisfying needs, and of making a long-term customer rather than a single sale.

The fourth and fifth views leave open the question for multinational companies as to *which* laws or conventional standards of morality are applicable to subsidiaries – those of the local country, or those of the country in which the company's headquarters are situated. The sixth view might lead to a conflict between the individual employee and the employer's expectations or requirements – although it is of course possible that an employee could have as a personal ethical standard 'business is business' and the employer something more 'social'. The seventh view, referred to in the following text as the *stakeholder model*, clearly conflicts with view number three, the *stockholder model*, which is still dominant in many countries.

Reading: Profits and social responsibility

Views 3, 4 and 5 are all expressed in the first long quotation from Milton Friedman. ('Ethical customs' means much the same thing as 'conventional standards of morality'.) View 7 is expressed in the final paragraph.

Friedman's article was published in *The New York Times Magazine*, 13 September 1970. Friedman expresses similar views at greater length in *Capitalism and Freedom* (Chicago: University of Chicago Press, 2002), originally published in 1962. The article is widely available on the Internet.

Comprehension

> ANSWERS
>
> 1 Because this is generally what the owners of the business want, and what they employ executives to do
> 2 The corporation's owners, the stockholders
> 3 The cost of socially responsible actions has to be paid in the form of lower dividends, higher prices, or lower wages
> 4 Because they involve doing things that should be done by governments, and if a government is not doing these things it is because the electors chose a government that did not say it was going to do them
> 5 A society with less pollution or less unemployment and fewer social problems

> 6 Any group of people with a stake in or an interest in or a claim on the business

Vocabulary

> **ANSWERS**
>
> 1 1 discrimination   2 undermining   3 free enterprise   4 conforming to   5 embodied   6 ethical   7 custom   8 insofar as   9 harms   10 proponents
> 2 avoid pollution, conduct business, conform to rules, eliminate discrimination, increase profits, make expenditures, make money, make profits, maximize profits, provide employment, undermine the basis

Discussion

As usual, there are few 'right answers' here.
- Whether doing anything other than maximizing profits is 'unbusinesslike' clearly depends on one's definition of business.
- It is probably true that stockholders *generally* wish to make as much money as possible, but many of them might well say something different if they were promised a trade-off such as lower dividends in return for less crime, or less polluted air, etc.
- It is quite difficult to argue against the statement that corporate social expenditure means spending someone else's money, given that the free enterprise, private-property system that Friedman describes is in operation in most countries; indeed a cynical description of management has long been 'spending other people's money'.
- That solving social problems is uniquely the job of the government needn't be true: Friedman neglects the fact that companies can always present their proposed 'social responsibility' policies for the approbation of their shareholders.
- Clearly someone who does *not* take an entirely capitalistic approach to business does not need to believe that the stockholders or shareholders are much more important than a company's other stakeholders. For example, there are obvious arguments *against* closing down a factory employing several hundred people in a small town with no other significant employers, and relocating production elsewhere in order to make small financial savings. This makes perfect business sense, but the resulting unemployment benefits have to be paid out of public tax revenues.

An additional **Writing** exercise would be to write short paragraphs (similar to the above), in opposition to the given arguments.

Listening 1: Socially responsible investment ▶ 2.17

AUDIO SCRIPT

ANNA-KIM HYUN-SEUNG   I see socially responsible investment as a very effective response to Milton Friedman's famous argument, because when Milton Friedman says 'The business of business is business,' it assumes that most shareholders want to maximize their profit, maximize their return on investment, and that is the goal of the shareholders. But what we can observe now is the rise of socially responsible investment, so it shows that at least some investors *do* care about social and environmental standards as well as their right to a return on investment. So if that's the case, if shareholders actually do care about these criteria, then Milton Friedman's argument is … is facing the serious problem of his assumptions, because it assumes that shareholders *only* care about the profit, and therefore corporations have to maximize the profit for their shareholders. But what if shareholders want something different for their corporations? It is true that socially responsible investment is still a fraction of the total investment at the moment, but is very very rapidly increasing, and it will be very interesting to see how the trend develops.

Economics

> **ANSWERS**
> 1 'The business of business is business', meaning that companies should only concentrate on doing business and making maximum profits
> 2 That the goal of shareholders is only to maximize their return on investment, or their profit
> 3 Only investing in companies that have certain social and environmental standards
> 4 It is currently only a fraction of the total amount of investment, but is increasing rapidly

Note

The kind of investment that Anna-Kim Hyun-Seung refers to here was mentioned in **Unit 16** – the 'Ethical growth fund' in the Case study.

Listening 2: Different stakeholder groups ▶ 2.18

AUDIO SCRIPT

ANNA-KIM HYUN-SEUNG I think it is very important to respond to different stakeholder groups, because obviously companies tend to be more responsive to the shareholders rather than other stakeholders, but I think when a company really considers different stakeholder groups seriously, including their community, including their own employees, then they are likely to have more genuine corporate social responsibility policies and practices.

For example, there are companies which are probably doing very good things for the community, for the external society, so that they can really improve their reputation with their external stakeholders, but for example, if they are not very nice to their own employees, if there is something going wrong within their supply chain management, with regard to human rights, low-cost child labour, working hours, then probably they don't really have a good response from their own employees, who are their own internal stakeholders, so I think it is very important to listen to all different stakeholders, internal and external, to develop a holistic approach to corporate social responsibility.

> **ANSWERS**
> 1 1 responsive 2 shareholders
>   3 community 4 employees 5 policies
>   6 practices 7 reputation 8 supply chain
>   9 human rights 10 child labour
> 2 Responding to both internal and external stakeholder groups, and not just the shareholders
> 3 Because if their employees, or their suppliers' employees, are badly treated, the company will not get the goodwill of its own employees

Discussion

As usual, this activity is best done in pairs or small groups, after which the answers can be discussed with the whole class.

There are clearly no definitive 'right answers', but here are some remarks:

1 Some people argue that where it is necessary to pay (i.e. bribe) someone to undertake some administrative work, or to do it more quickly, this is equivalent to paying for a service, and is not the same as bribing people in order to win business contracts.
2 Companies are recommended to do *benchmarking* – going outside the company to discover the best practices in an industry, and copying them – but this does *not* generally include industrial espionage!
3 Like the concept *caveat emptor*, built-in obsolescence clearly conflicts with the modern marketing logic of satisfying faithful customers. However, if products last too long …
4 Some people have gone as far as describing political power (a consequence of lobbying) as 'the fifth P of marketing'.
5 Most countries have legislation concerning seriously misleading advertising. The same objection can be made to telling only half the truth in advertising, or exaggerating a great deal, or keeping quiet about bad aspects of products as can be made to built-in obsolescence: it conflicts with the marketing logic of creating long-term customers. Yet the advertising for products that people pay for only once will always tend to exaggerate, e.g. people are unlikely to stop going to the cinema because they dislike one misleadingly advertised movie. And chocolate manufacturers, for

example, are unlikely to mention in their advertising that their product is probably bad for your teeth, your weight, and your skin complexion.

6 Whistle-blowers are likely to be dismissed for breach of contract; a question which often arises is whether they deserve legal protection or compensation.

Role play: Problems at a clothes manufacturer

There are five role cards at the back of the Student's Book on pages 146, 149, 151, 152 and 154. The situation here involves two potentially ethical dilemmas: whether to lay off staff and whether to continue to use a polluting chemical.

It is essential that the chair follows the instructions, and speaks first, followed by the Chief Scientist, before allowing the other participants to speak.

The outcome is unpredictable. While the Human Resources Manager's arguments may be implausible, a similar authentic outcome is mentioned in **Unit 25** on Efficiency and employment. The Financial Manager (of course!) gets the 'bad', unethical role, but some learners may agree. The Marketing Manager's 'wikinomic' suggestion (see **Unit 4**) may well find favour, but this doesn't solve the over-production and employment problem.

Vocabulary notes

Some words from the role cards, which can be clarified, if necessary, after the learners have read their roles:

Sewers /ˈsəʊəz/ meaning people who *sew* /səʊ/ (make pieces of clothing with needles and thread) is not to be confused with its homograph *sewers* /ˈsuːəz/, meaning underground pipes used for carrying waste water and human waste away from bathrooms and toilets to sewage works where it is treated. (Similarly, *sew* is not to be confused with its homophone *sow* /səʊ/ meaning to put seeds in the ground so that plants will grow, while this meaning of *sow* is not to be confused with its homograph *sow* /saʊ/, meaning an adult female pig, etc.!)

Fabric, meaning a type of cloth or woven material, is not to be confused with the word meaning *factory* in many European languages (*Fabrik, fabriek, fabrique, fabbrica, fábrica,* etc.).

Selling point, meaning a characteristic of a product that makes it attractive to potential customers, is not to be confused with *point of sale*, the location where something is purchased.

Odour (BrE), meaning smell, is spelt – or spelled (AmE) – *odor* in AmE.

See also the simulations 'Smoke Signals', 'A Pirate's Dilemma', and 'Dirty Work' in *Decisionmaker* by David Evans (Cambridge University Press).

25 Efficiency and employment

This unit considers the trade-off between business efficiency and employment: increased efficiency generally leads to job losses. There are the usual opening discussion questions, followed by vocabulary exercises covering the key terms. These are followed by listening exercises based on an example from South Korea, and a role play involving a postal service that wants to restructure its sorting offices.

Lead-in

Job security was also discussed in the Lead-in to **Unit 2**. Business students are generally more interested in things like a challenging job than security. Most will probably say they expect to change employers several times, except entrepreneurial types, who may deny that they will ever work for anyone else!

The idea of a 'work portfolio', consisting of several different contracts rather than a full-time job or a lifelong career, was popularized by Charles Handy's well-known book *The Age of Unreason* (Harvard Business School Press, 1990). If flexible organizations offer fewer full-time positions, it becomes the individual's responsibility to create job opportunities. Yet many people, if not most, still seem to prefer to do a single full-time job.

The answer to the question about whether technological progress creates or destroys jobs probably depends on the industry and the country; this Teacher's Book does *not* have any figures to offer.

> *Fire* and *sack* often mean to be dismissed because the person has done something wrong; *lay off* and *make redundant* are more often used when members of staff are no longer necessary; to *let go* is a euphemism for to *lay off*.
>
> **3** **1** contract work   **2** Job sharing
> **3** delayering   **4** outsourced or contracted out, relocate or delocalize   **5** downsized or rightsized or restructured, redundant

Vocabulary notes

Down-sizing, *right-sizing* and *de-layering* can also be hyphenated, especially in BrE; *jobsharing* can also be written as one word.

The terms *upsizing* and *resizing* are occasionally used when an organization increases the number of staff employed.

Vocabulary

> **ANSWERS**
>
> **1** **1** flexible labour market   **2** downsizing
> **3** outsourcing or contracting-out
> **4** job sharing   **5** relocation or delocalization
> **6** delayering   **7** rationalization or restructuring
> **8** contract work   **9** casual work   **10** rightsizing
>
> **2** *appoint*, *engage*, *hire*, *recruit* and *take on* mean to employ; *fire*, *lay off*, *let go*, *make redundant* and *sack* mean to dismiss
>
> *Appoint* and *engage* are generally used for senior positions; *hire* and *take on* are more often used when companies employ large numbers of new staff.
>
> *Recruit* means to hire people, sometimes with the sense that they have to be persuaded to join (as with army recruiting offices).

Discussion

Cases of restructuring or downsizing or delocalizing are generally met with dismay about job losses, except by those whose interest is in efficiency and profit.

Concerning the possible solutions to unemployment:
- people with interesting and responsible jobs are often opposed to sharing them with someone else. For example, if you are a brand manager, or the person responsible for dealing with particular clients, investors, or investments, you probably don't want to spend Thursday and Friday at home worrying about what someone else is doing with 'your' job. It is also more expensive for companies to hire two part-time workers for the same job
- people in boring jobs would probably be happy with a cut in working hours, but not with the consequent reduction of income

- retiring at a younger age, or working fewer years in one's life, perhaps taking some years off, for example when your children are young, as many women already do, equally involve a reduction of income. The burden on current workers to pay the pensions of the previous generation is already increasing; many countries want to raise the retirement age
- training programmes are presumably a good idea if there are or will be jobs available that require the skills of the newly trained workers, but some unemployed people still have few skills and lack the capacities to learn others
- public sector jobs obviously have to be paid for out of tax revenue.

Listening 1: Efficiency and the number of employees ▶ 2.19

AUDIO SCRIPT

ANNA-KIM HYUN-SEUNG Increasing business efficiency doesn't necessarily conflict with the interests of employees, although that is often the case. In most cases companies probably just want to lower the number of employees when they increase their efficiency. But I know of a few companies which managed to increase their efficiency but they actually, instead of going for lay-offs, instead of reducing the number of employees, they actually decided to reduce the average number of working hours per employee, so that the employees can invest their time in training, development, education, arguably even leading to a better quality of life, and work and life balance, especially at the factory level, at the shop-floor level. So, there are cases that actually achieve both increasing efficiency and maintaining the benefits for employees. But of course that's probably only a few examples.

ANSWERS

1 Reduce their number of employees
2 Reducing the average number of working hours per employee, so that the employees can spend time on training, development and education
3 They had a better quality of life, and a better work/life balance, and become more efficient at work

Listening 2: Efficiency, training and productivity ▶ 2.20

AUDIO SCRIPT

ANNA-KIM HYUN-SEUNG I have one example which is a Korean company. It's called Yuhan-Kimberly and it's a form of joint venture between Yuhan, a local company, and Kimberly Clark in the United States. So Yuhan-Kimberly is itself a local player, they are the market leader in their industry, they make toilet paper, tissues, and sanitary items. Within South Korea they are probably one of the most respected companies because of their very consistent corporate social responsibility policies and practice. For example, in 1984, they launched the very first nationwide environmental campaigning, which was about developing forests. The company really tried to commit themselves in social and responsible causes.

I don't exactly remember the year, but at some point the company had problems and they had the situation that they needed to cut down the total number of working hours, and what they chose was instead of cutting down the number of employees they cut down the number of average working hours, so they actually changed their shift system. Before the change it was three teams, three shifts, but they changed it into four teams, two shifts, and I think each worker worked consecutively four days, 48 hours, 12 hours each day, and they took off four days, and one of the four days was committed to a training programme operated by the company. It was part of their lifelong learning programme as well, so I think the employees responded in very good ways because for them it was obviously a much better choice than losing their job, and it was also a training opportunity. Also after this change there was a big increase in productivity because obviously the workers could have the proper rest for three or four days.

ANSWERS

1 They make toilet paper, tissues, and sanitary items in South Korea, in a joint venture with the American company Kimberly Clark.

Economics

2 They have a long history of socially responsible corporate policies and practices.
3 They cut the number of average working hours rather than cutting the number of employees. Everyone worked four 12-hour shifts and then took four days off, one of which was spent on a training programme.
4 The workers responded well and there was a big increase in productivity as the workers were properly rested.

The answer to the discussion question is that this situation *is* rather exceptional, which is why Anna-Kim Hyun-Seung remembers and cites it. It probably requires total confidence that sales will increase again and that the workers will all be needed in the long term.

Discussion: The postal service

In many countries, postal services were traditionally a nationalized monopoly, often combined with telephone services, and often inefficient from a business perspective, but there is a growing trend towards privatization, especially of telephone and banking services.

At the time of writing, the Royal Mail in Britain is a limited company owned by the government, but it is expected to be partly privatized. The United States Postal Service is an independent government agency, and the third biggest employer in the country (after the Department of Defense and Wal-Mart).

Postal services that are considered to be a public service rather than a source of profit often have unprofitable small post offices in thinly-populated areas, which generally come under threat of closure if the organization is privatized. Whether everyone should have access to a local post office is a matter of opinion, and an issue that generally separates the political left and right – and people living in urban and rural areas.

Role play: Reorganizing the postal service

Reading

This situation is fairly closely based on events in Switzerland a few years ago. The plan naturally met with a lot of opposition from trade unions and left-wing parties, and was badly received by many journalists. The post office swiftly compromised, and established several geographically dispersed secondary sorting centres as well as the three main ones.

Comprehension

ANSWERS

1 They want to reduce the number of sorting offices from 25 to three large, new, efficient, automated ones.
2 Because it is necessary to become more efficient and competitive in a future open market with international competition. They are also facing a continuing decrease in the volume of mail.
3 The main advantage would be cost savings due to rationalization; the main disadvantages are that 4,500 people would lose their jobs, and many of the 5,500 people who retained their jobs would have longer journeys to work and would have to work at night.
4 The trade unions and local governments where sorting offices would be closed are against the plan; local governments in the areas where the three new centres are planned are in favour of the project.

Role play

There are four role cards at the back of the Student's Book on pages 147, 149, 151 and 153. As usual, the learners can first discuss and prepare their roles in pairs or small groups. As always, it is necessary to select a competent learner to take the role of the CEO who chairs the meeting. The four participants should speak in the order indicated.

Given the four roles, if there is a vote to close the meeting the most probable outcome is a 2–2 tie, but persuasive speakers may be able to sway others and change their minds.

Writing

No model answer is given, as the outcome of the meeting is uncertain. The learners could look at the information in the role cards in the Student's Book to help them write their summary.

Efficiency and employment **Unit 25** 111

26 Exchange rates

This unit contains a text outlining the recent history of exchange rates, and reasons why they fluctuate, listening exercises on a proposed tax on international currency transactions, and a case study about such a tax.

Lead-in

An **additional first question**: Quickly – how many currencies can you name in 30 seconds, starting NOW?!

For Europeans, naming different currencies was easier before the introduction of the euro, but so it goes! Lists of currencies are easily available on the Internet.

The traditional reasons for buying foreign currencies were for foreign travel and international trade – buying goods or services from abroad. Today, as is explained in the Reading text, 95% of currency transactions are purely speculative. Organizations and individuals buy foreign currencies to get higher interest rates or hoping to make a short-term capital gain if the other currency appreciates.

Today, exchange rates are generally determined by market forces (supply and demand) – the quantities bought and sold.

Learners who have travelled may know about exchange rate fluctuations, and most business students should too!

Reading: Exchange rates

You could also attempt to elicit much of the information given in the text with the learners' books closed, by asking questions.

The system of pegging against the US dollar and against gold, mentioned in the first paragraph, was known as the 'Bretton Woods system' after an international conference held in a small town in New Hampshire in 1944. The Bretton Woods Conference also led to the establishment of the World Bank and the International Monetary Fund the following year.

Since the end of gold convertibility, a dollar is merely a piece of paper on which is written 'In God We Trust': God, not gold!

The day the Bank of England lost billions of pounds is known as 'Black Wednesday' (16 September 1992). The Conservative government was forced to withdraw the pound from the European Exchange Rate Mechanism, as they were not able to keep sterling above its agreed lower limit. One of the people active in the markets that day was the financier George Soros, who made over US$1 billion profit by selling sterling – or rather by short-selling it: selling currency he did not own at the time of the sale, but which he purchased later at a lower price. He gave some of the proceeds to a foundation that set up English language schools in central and eastern Europe.

> **ANSWERS**
>
> The paragraph headings come in this order:
> B C E A D

Comprehension

> **SUGGESTED ANSWERS (OR MORE PRECISELY, QUESTIONS)**
>
> 1 What was gold convertibility?
> 2 Why did gold convertibility end in 1971?
> 3 How is a floating exchange rate determined?
> 4 What would happen if there was purchasing power parity? *or* What would happen if currencies were correctly valued?
> 5 Why do speculators buy foreign currencies?
> 6 What proportion of currency transactions are speculative?
> 7 How can companies try to protect themselves against currency fluctuations?
> 8 How can governments attempt to influence the value of their currency?
> 9 Why are governments' or central banks' attempts to influence exchange rates not very successful?

Economics

Vocabulary

> **ANSWERS**
>
> 1 revalue   2 devalue   3 floating
> 4 proponents   5 depreciate   6 appreciate
> 7 hedge   8 fluctuations   9 futures contracts

Discussion

- At the time of writing (June 2009), the price of gold is about $950 an ounce. This could easily change.
- The quantity of the US currency currently backed by gold is less than 1%. At the other extreme, until 2000, there was a legal requirement that a minimum of 40% of Swiss francs had to be backed by gold reserves; the figure is now less than 20%. Figures for other countries may be available on the Internet.
- The main argument against government or central bank intervention in currency markets is that it is generally unproductive, because currency speculators can counteract the (small) effect it has.
- The most obvious way to discourage currency speculation would be a tax on currency transactions. Whether currency speculators should be prevented or taxed is the subject of the following Listening activity.

Listening 1: Currency flows and the Tobin Tax ▶ 2.21

> **AUDIO SCRIPT**
>
> **MICHAEL KITSON** ... it's very difficult of course to intervene, to regulate exchange rates, because now they're changing very very quickly. Money is flowing instantaneously backwards and forwards, it's what many people call 'hot money'. Money flowing in another country quickly, and in and out of a country quickly, and it has been, arguably, helped to deepen financial crises, such as the south-east Asian crisis in the end of the 1990s, when money flew out of these economies, and money can flow very quickly and destabilize, and we should add that then leads to real effects, real effects I mean people lose jobs, unemployment goes up, and output falls. So we've got this problem of these, of money flowing in and out of countries. Can we regulate it? Well, it's very difficult, but there are arguments that perhaps we can, or certainly arguments to consider.
>
> Now one, for instance, is something called the Tobin Tax. Now the Tobin Tax is an argument you tax, at a very small rate, 0.01, or 0.1, very small tax on currency purchase and currency selling. OK. Now, what that would do is should dampen down currency speculation, because remember what people are doing in terms of currency flows is they're ... they're buying and selling currencies with very small differences, OK, you spend, you buy and sell currencies, a big volume of currency, on a small difference to make you money. Sometimes it's called 'highly leveraged' – you borrow a lot of money – to buy a currency or sell a currency. If you make a small tax, you may discourage people from buying and selling so rapidly, and just dampen down those currency fluctuations.
>
> I may add, a Tobin Tax will not prevent a major crisis, but may dampen down the currency speculation over time. Now the Tobin Tax, which was suggested by a Nobel Prize winner, James Tobin, who I think thought it was a theoretical issue and perhaps wasn't ... wouldn't be practical. Many have argued it just wouldn't be possible to implement this Tobin Tax, but what's interesting as the world economy's developed, as exchange rates have suffered from crises, increasingly people are thinking it's back on the agenda. OK, we need to reconsider, perhaps the Tobin Tax would be possible in certain circumstances, and perhaps with ICT – information technology – we could coordinate it at a global level.
>
> One country cannot introduce a Tobin Tax because then other, all the trading would take place elsewhere. It has to take place globally ... but now we say that actually we can have a global system of regulation, the ICT may actually now facilitate it, and we can actually implement this sort of policy.

> **ANSWERS**
>
> 1 Speculative money that is invested in a currency for a very short time

2 Increased unemployment and falling output
3 A very small tax on currency purchase and currency selling, designed to reduce currency speculation
4 Buying or selling currency with borrowed money
5 It would probably reduce or 'dampen down' currency trading and currency fluctuations.
6 ICT (information and communication technology) makes global coordination possible.

Notes

The south-east Asian financial crisis that Michael Kitson refers to occurred in 1997. The value of various currencies collapsed dramatically, especially in Thailand, South Korea and Indonesia.

Kitson talks about money *flowing* in and out of countries, and then about how money *flew* out of south-east Asia. These are of course two different verbs: *flow – flowed; fly – flew – flown*.

Kitson uses the numbers 0.01 and 0.1, which he says as *nought point nought one* and *nought point one*. This is a British usage; Americans would say *zero* instead of *nought*.

Listening 2: Developing Africa

AUDIO SCRIPT

MICHAEL KITSON   And the other argument of course is, it's a very small tax but it will raise a significant amount of revenue.

What would you do with that? Again, another issue. One of the arguments, you could use that revenue to go to the parts of the world where the world economy does not invest. OK, it doesn't make sense for individual investors in most cases to put lots of money into, say, Africa, to build up infrastructure, roads and education, which will help to develop that region of the world. But you could use the resources generated from a Tobin Tax, which would generate significant, significant social benefits for Africa, and significant economic benefits for the region and the world economy as a whole. It would be a world tax and a world expenditure, and you'd spend it where the world economy and the depressed regions would benefit most.

I mean, I don't think you can criticize individual firms for not investing in Africa, because they won't get what they call a private rate of return, they will not make profit from it, but there's a significant social rate of return – better education, better economic growth, better standards of living, people living longer. OK, we need to think about how we're going to get those resources into Africa, I think it's one of the great challenges.

ANSWERS

1 Because they won't get a sufficient rate of return, or a profit
2 Africa would get a significant social rate of return: better education, better economic growth, better standards of living, longer life expectancy, etc.

Case study: A currency transaction tax

The figures given in the Student's Book come from Rodney Schmidt, *The Currency Transaction Tax: Rate and Revenue Estimates* (Tokyo, New York and Paris: United Nations University Press, 2008): http://tinyurl.com/ycse2rs (consulted October 2009).

Several organizations which support a Tobin Tax or other currency transaction tax have websites which provide further information.

Additional preliminary discussion questions could be:
- Do you agree that currency transactions should be taxed, and not, e.g. stock market transactions?
- Are there any alternative ways of raising money internationally (e.g. a carbon tax)?

The learners can discuss the questions in small groups, and then share their decisions with the whole class.

Although alternative energy is one of the suggestions, this topic is covered in greater detail in **Unit 28**.

Writing

This activity could be done either individually, or collaboratively as a group.

27 International trade

This unit contains two listening sections in which Michael Kitson talks about the theory of free trade and comparative advantage, and infant industries and strategic industries, an extract from an interview with the Korean economist Ha-Joon Chang about infant industries, and a reading and discussion section about the advantages and disadvantages of free trade and the policies of the World Trade Organization.

Lead-in

Much of the audio-visual and computing equipment in a classroom is likely to have been imported, as well, probably, as teaching materials. Most of the learners' clothes and shoes were probably produced abroad. And so on.

Many countries would like to restrict imports, to protect their balance of trade, and their own producers, but in a customs union such as the EU (European Union) or NAFTA (the North American Free Trade Agreement) this is impossible. Furthermore, most countries are members of the WTO (World Trade Organization), which tries to remove obstacles or barriers to international trade.

Vocabulary

ANSWERS
1 I   2 C   3 D   4 B   5 A   6 G   7 H   8 E   9 F

Listening 1: Free trade ▶ 2.23

AUDIO SCRIPT

MICHAEL KITSON   I think I would argue that many economists favour free trade, and some governments see the problems with free trade, under certain circumstances. We all know that economics is based on simplified models. And sometimes those simplified models are not useful in explaining the way the real world works, or sometimes there are exceptions to those models.

Let's take into account the standard argument for free trade – OK, that everybody gets better off, more efficiency, we can consume more goods and services. Well, that may be the case, but there may be some people who lose out. Take the very simple argument, we often have two economies with two goods, OK, we simplify and then we extend. So say we've got two economies with two goods. We've got a developed country producing computers and cloth, and we have an underdeveloped country that's trying to produce computers and cloth. OK, and then we say, well actually with free trade you should specialize in what you're best at, or least worst at. OK, so under that situation we say, right, to the developed country, you produce computers, and sell some computers to the developing country, and the developing country, you focus on cloth, and buy the computers from the developed country, and so on. That's our standard model, OK. And we can see that there's efficiency gains, ultimately we should be able to get, consume more computers and cloth through that process.

But let's think what happens there. I'm working in a cloth factory in a developed country. We move from going from no trade to free trade. My country specializes just in computers. What's going to happen, I'm going to lose my job. OK. Now that may be a big concern, governments may be concerned about workers losing jobs in certain sectors. Now we could argue in theory I just need to reallocate my job and become working in computing. It may be very difficult for me to do that. I may be in the wrong part of the country, I may not have the right skills and so on.

Basically what happens with free trade is that many many people gain and a few people may lose and they may lose big time, and if we're concerned about those people we may want to have some transition process, we may be concerned about unfettered free trade.

> **SUGGESTED ANSWERS**
>
> 1 They are simplified, and not always useful in explaining how the real world works, and sometimes there are exceptions
> 2 Everyone becomes better off, there is more efficiency, and we can consume more goods and services
> 3 A developed country producing both computers and cloth, and an underdeveloped country that's trying to produce computers and cloth
> 4 Workers in a cloth factory in a developed country who lose their jobs, and who might find it very difficult to get new jobs, because they are in the wrong part of the country, or don't have the right skills
> 5 Some kind of transition process (between no trade and free trade)

Notes

Kitson also uses the expression 'unfettered free trade' in **Unit 22**, where *unfettered* (meaning not limited by any rules or controls) is in a vocabulary exercise.

The fourth question could also be answered in the singular, as Kitson talks about a single worker.

Cloth of course means a textile or a type of woven material, not *clothes*.

The model that Kitson describes, and the theory of comparative advantage, were put forward by David Ricardo in *Principles of Political Economy and Taxation* (1817), following on from Adam Smith's account of specialization or the division of labour, and the advantages of free markets and free trade in *An Inquiry into the Nature and Causes of the Wealth of Nations* (1776).

Listening 2: Exceptions to free trade
▶ 2.24

> **AUDIO SCRIPT**
>
> **MICHAEL KITSON**   OK, so that's case number one. OK, that some people may lose out and we may be concerned about protecting them. Let's go back to our free trade example. Now we've got our one country specializing in computers and another country specializing in cloth. Now that cloth-producing country may say OK, that's our comparative advantage, cloth, but we don't want to remain cloth producers for the rest of our … in the future, we want our country to develop and grow. We want to produce a wider range of goods and services, or goods and services that are higher value added. And it would generate higher wages and economic growth. We want to move out of cloth into something else. We want to move out of cloth into automobiles and perhaps into computing in the longer term. How are we going to do that with our comparative advantage just being cloth? We may need to protect certain sectors of our economy to let them grow.
>
> There's a very good argument in economics called the infant industry argument. OK, we establish these industries, and they're new and young, they cannot compete with the bigger more established industries in the advanced countries. We need to leave them time to develop and grow, and then they can compete with other countries. So we need to protect those sectors, so they can grow and we can have a new comparative advantage in the future. So I think under those circumstances we can have arguments where you may want to not have unfettered free trade.
>
> Now let's think about advanced countries. Advanced countries, arguably, mainly focus on free trade and the advantages of free trade, but even here we can have arguments about why you want to, why you want to support or protect certain sectors. This is sometimes called strategic trade theory. OK, we can identify strategic sectors of the economy. Those sectors may benefit other parts of the economy. It's what economists call externalities. Externalities basically means, a positive externality, something in one part of the economy may have positive benefits elsewhere. OK, or those sectors may generate economies of scale, so as you protect them they become bigger and more competitive. Say, for instance, we say aerospace, it's crucial to have an aerospace industry. Why?

Because the knowledge generated in aerospace will ... will go elsewhere, be porous. The ideas generated in aerospace will go into automotive, will go into electrical engineering, go into other sectors, so if we have a strong aerospace sector, it will benefit the rest of the economy. That may be an argument for protecting that sector, under certain circumstances.

> **SUGGESTED ANSWERS**
>
> 1 Because other goods and services have a higher value added and would generate higher wages and economic growth.
> 2 Protecting the new sectors of the economy to let them develop and grow, until they have a comparative advantage and can compete with other countries.
> 3 They may generate economies of scale, and benefit other parts of the economy (by way of positive externalities).
> 4 Aerospace, which generates knowledge that goes into the automotive industry (motor vehicles), electrical engineering, etc.

Reading: Education and protection

The South Korean economist Ha-Joon Chang, a professor at the University of Cambridge, is the author of several books, including *Kicking Away the Ladder: Development Strategy in Historical Perspective* (London: Anthem Press, 2002), which points out that almost all of today's rich countries used tariff protection and subsidies to develop their industries, but now urge free-market, free-trade policies. In *Bad Samaritans – Rich Nations, Poor Policies, and the Threat to the Developing World* (London: Random House, 2007), he argues that the International Monetary Fund, the World Bank, and wealthy countries are holding back development and creating poverty. This book has been republished with different subtitles: the British paperback is called *Bad Samaritans – The Guilty Secrets of Rich Nations and the Threat to Global Prosperity* (Random House, 2008), and the US edition is *Bad Samaritans – The Myth of Free Trade and the Secret History of Capitalism* (New York: Bloomsbury Press, 2008).

The text in the Student's Book is extracted from an interview, available at: http://www.multinationalmonitor.org/mm2008/092008/interview-chang.html (consulted June 2009).

This extract from the interview is similar to the beginning of Chapter 3 of *Bad Samaritans*. Elsewhere in the book, Chang offers a counter argument to the globalization theories of Thomas L. Friedman (see **Unit 8: Production**).

Additional questions: What is the minimum school-leaving age in your country? How long has it been like this? What was it 100 or 150 years ago?

The minimum school-leaving age in developed countries is generally at least 16, but this is a relatively recent state of affairs. In Britain, for example, education only became compulsory in 1870, between the ages of 5 and 12. In other words, children began work just after their 12th birthday, although exceptions were made in agricultural areas to start even earlier. The leaving age was gradually raised to 16 during the following 100 years.

(Another additional question: Why doesn't Chang include business manager or language teacher in his list of desirable jobs?!)

> **SUGGESTED ANSWERS**
>
> 1 The analogy is that although children *could* start unskilled work at a very young age (and learn how to be productive, because of competition), they need many years of education if they are ever going to get a good, well-paid job; similarly, to develop advanced industries which give a high return, it is necessary to protect them while they grow up and increase their efficiency and productivity.
> 2 The short-term disadvantage is that consumers have to use expensive, inferior products from inefficient domestic producers, rather than be free to buy superior imported goods.

Discussion

- In answer to the first question, learners may suggest either potentially strategic industries, or potential infant industries, depending on what country they are from.
- The second question (or questions) might lead to a conflict between agreeing with Chang's argument theoretically, and not wanting to spend hard-earned money (or indeed a student grant!) on inferior or more expensive goods (or food), especially if there is a risk that the infant industry might fail.

Vocabulary

This short exercise contains words from the activity which follows. Many learners will know the word *dumping*, which exists as a loan word in many, if not most, European languages.

> **ANSWERS**
>
> **1** generic   **2** trademark   **3** dumping
> **4** copyright   **5** subsidize

Reading and discussion: For and against free trade

Information on the World Trade Organization is readily available on the Internet, notably on the WTO's own site, http://www.wto.org. Anti-WTO sites can be found by searching for 'anti-WTO' or 'against the WTO', etc.

Some learners may have very strong views on this subject, which could lead to lively discussion.

Although the Student's Book asks 'Which set of arguments do you find the most convincing?', and the following activity requires learners to prepare a brief talk or a written report summarizing the arguments either in favour of or against free trade, many learners may find some arguments on both sides convincing. In this case, an alternative activity would be to classify in order the eight or ten most persuasive statements or arguments.

Another way of finding claims to agree and disagree with would be to type 'globalization means' and 'globalisation means' into Google (separately; it won't look for both at once) and look at the extracts given, or at a few of the sites. For example, a quick search in June 2009 came up with:

- Globalisation means countries can prosper from worldwide recession – if they are smart
- Globalisation means job losses for unionised labour
- Globalisation means new challenges for sustainability
- Globalisation means no barriers to money but razor wire for refugees
- Globalization means accepting people's distinct identities
- Globalization Means Consumer Power
- Globalization means integration of peoples, integration of religions, tolerance and dialogue between peoples and religions
- Globalization means reconnecting the human community
- Globalization means the breakdown of boundaries as barriers to economic exploitation
- Globalization means uprooting old ways of life and threatening livelihoods and cultures

This idea comes from an article which has nothing to do with language teaching: Wolfgang Teubert, 'Parole-linguistics and the diachronic dimension of the discourse', in *Text, Discourse and Corpora: Theory and Analysis* by Michael Hoey, Michaela Mahlberg, Michael Stubbs and Wolfgang Teubert (London: Continuum, 2007).

> **ANSWERS**
>
> In favour: A   C   E   F   I   J   L
> Against: B   D   G   H   K   M   N

Presentation

This could be prepared in pairs or small groups. Unlike the Presentation in **Unit 22**, which asked learners to consider arguments on both sides of a question, the objective here is to prepare a forceful but one-sided argument.

The learners' presentations are likely to be quite similar, so probably only a few should be offered to the whole class. However, the learners could all prepare a written version out of class.

28 Economics and ecology

This unit is about global warming and the economic consequences of energy policy. It contains an extract from an article by an economist arguing that we should prioritize reducing poverty rather than fighting global warming, and extracts from an interview with a climate scientist about environmental policy and climate change. There is a role play about making energy policy recommendations for a developing country.

Lead-in

- As most learners can be expected to know, global warming is largely caused by the burning of carbon-based fuels, which release carbon dioxide into the atmosphere. You may, however, have a learner who insists that this is not true, and that it is caused by changes in the sun, or some such, which would at least enliven this discussion activity.
- Possible solutions include reducing the use of carbon-based energy, and replacing it with solar power, wind power, hybrid petrol-electric cars, etc. Some of these solutions are being implemented, but not at a rate fast enough to slow down, let alone reverse, climate change. Many governments are unwilling to take measures that will reduce their country's economic growth and standard of living.
- An international response to global warming would obviously be preferable, but learners may have differing views as to what individual countries could or should do. A mixed class may be able to outline the situation in their different countries.
- Some learners will (claim to) have changed the way they live because of an awareness of climate change and their 'carbon footprint', and be conscientious in paying carbon offsetting charges, etc; others may look mystified! I'm told that wearing high-heeled shoes on aeroplanes to reduce your carbon footprint does *not* work!

Reading: The economics of climate change

Christian Gollier is the Director of the Laboratoire d'Economie des Ressources Naturelles of the Institut d'Economie Industrielle of the Université des Sciences Sociales in Toulouse, France.

His article 'The Economics of Climate Change: A Critical Analysis of the Stern Review' was published by the OECD (Organisation for Economic Co-operation and Development) in 2007, at http://www.oecd.org/dataoecd/32/4/40133781.pdf (consulted April 2009). The text is made up of short extracts, without the ellipses indicated.

The Stern Review on the Economics of Climate Change was commissioned by the UK government, and published in 2006. It was led by Lord Stern, at the time the Head of the Government Economic Service and a former World Bank Chief Economist.

> **ANSWER**
>
> He says that fighting poverty is more important than cutting CO_2 emissions.

Comprehension

> **ANSWERS**
>
> 1 Because most of the consequences will not appear before the year 2100, and the people living then will be much wealthier than us, and so will be able to do something then
> 2 Because the future value of money spent today has to be discounted by the rate of return of capital over the intervening period
> 3 Spending money on fighting malaria, and improving access to clean drinking water
> 4 It will force them to spend some of the benefits of their economic growth on things other than fighting poverty (which should be the first priority)

Vocabulary

> **ANSWERS**
>
> 1 1 mean 2 bear 3 stemming from 4 crucial question 5 discounted 6 rate of return (of capital) 7 In a nutshell 8 highly cost-effective 9 poorest nations (or developing nations) 10 poverty line
>
> 2 bear costs, benefit people, cut CO_2 emissions, cut costs, cut poverty, discount benefits, discount costs, fight global warming, fight poverty, help people, implement policies, redistribute wealth, reduce CO_2 emissions, reduce costs, reduce global warming, reduce (the) impact (of)

Vocabulary note

Bear is an irregular verb (*bear – bore – borne*); the past participle *borne* appears later in the text.

Discussion

It is true that people in poor countries suffering from malaria and without clean drinking water have higher priorities than cutting carbon dioxide emissions, but most people think that climate change will have serious effects on the planet long before the date Gollier gives, 2100.

Some learners may be appalled by this argument; the following Listening activity gives a contrary viewpoint.

Vocabulary

An **additional discussion question** would be to ask what point the cartoonist was trying to make. [Presumably that hybrid or electric cars, whose owners often feel very virtuous, are not really an advance if the electricity they use comes from burning carbon (or specifically coal, as in the cartoon).]

> **ANSWERS**
>
> 1 1 A 2 C 3 J 4 I 5 E 6 H 7 D 8 B 9 F 10 K 11 G

Notes

This is the sense of *inertia* used in Listening 3 below; the word also has other meanings which are almost the contrary. The *Cambridge Advanced Learner's Dictionary* gives:

> **inertia** (FORCE) the physical force that keeps something in the same position or moving in the same direction
>
> **inertia** (LACK OF ACTIVITY) lack of activity or interest, or unwillingness to make an effort to do anything

> **ANSWERS**
>
> 2 a *decrease, diminish, drop, dwindle, fall, recede, shrink* and *shrivel* all mean to become smaller
>   b *augment, expand, extend, grow, increase, inflate, multiply, rise* and *swell* all mean to become bigger

Listening 1: A big step forward ▶ 2.25

The interview with Martin Beniston was not recorded by a professional sound recordist, and the quality is not as good as most of the other Listenings.

> **AUDIO SCRIPT**
>
> **MARTIN BENISTON** Well, as a climate scientist I feel we are moving forward in the right direction, albeit too slowly in terms of some of the urgent issues that need to be addressed in terms of climate change. But certainly, compared to 10 or 15 years ago, climate change is now on the agenda of policy, it's on the agenda of large companies, who are thinking ahead in terms of remaining competitive while at the same time addressing energy and climate issues, so I think there has been a big step forward. On the other hand, one still sees many declarations, like the G8 Declaration, which looked very promising, but whether anybody is actually going to put that into effect within the proposed timeframe is another matter. And it's not just a matter of political will, it's also … is the technology there to help us along, and so on and so forth. What's going to happen with the emerging economic giants like China and India, who are sort of not

too keen on going ahead with this, and China's almost on a par with the United States now in terms of its global carbon emissions, so it's a huge actor in the game, and if China doesn't come in, and India doesn't come in, then we're going to be in trouble.

> **SUGGESTED ANSWERS**
>
> 1 Both governments and large companies are now addressing urgent energy and climate issues
> 2 There is no guarantee that the G8 Declaration will be put into effect, or that the necessary technology will be available,
> 3 As emerging economic giants
> 4 They are not very keen on the G8's proposals, but there will be problems if they don't accept them (as China is now responsible for almost as many carbon emissions as the United States).

Note

The G8 Declaration to which Beniston refers is 'Responsible Leadership for a Sustainable Future', L'Aquila, Italy, July 2009.

The G8 leaders (US, Japan, Germany, France, UK, Italy, Canada, Russia) agreed that the global average temperature should not be more than 2° higher than pre-industrial levels, and that there should be a 50% global reduction of greenhouse gas emissions (GHGs) by 2050. The Declaration also said that developed countries should reduce their emissions 'by 80% or more by 2050 compared to 1990 or more recent years'. See http://tinyurl.com/ncno2t/ (consulted October 2009).

Official statistics state that China's emissions are now higher than the USA's.

Listening 2: Emerging technologies
▶ 2.26

As there are ten gaps to complete in question 1, you could perhaps play the extract normally the first time, and then play it a second time, briefly pausing the CD once or twice, e.g. at the end of the first and second sentences.

AUDIO SCRIPT

MARTIN BENISTON   Well, I think if we look at all the emerging technologies related to sort of green energy and other environmentally friendly technologies, it's certainly more of an opportunity than a hindrance. I think much of the reticence of politicians up till now, and the general public to some extent, related to the climate change issue was that one had the impression that, you know, to try and become carbon neutral, or to try and revert … reverse the, you know, global warming, would mean going back to the Stone Age or to the Middle Ages or something, you know, this is not really the case, I mean it's not at all the case. And certainly there are huge opportunities out there for, you know, transform the economy, and transformations of technology, and so on, so I would say … in fact if you look at some of the more progressive countries towards environmentally-friendly technologies you do see that GDP has actually grown in places like Denmark, while at the same time carbon emissions have not progressed at all and have even dwindled to some extent, the same for Sweden even if the Swedish case is less spectacular, so it does show that you can decouple carbon emissions from economic growth, so why not take that route?

> **ANSWERS**
>
> 1 1 green energy   2 environmentally friendly
>   3 hindrance   4 reticence   5 carbon neutral
>   6 opportunities   7 GDP   8 emissions
>   9 dwindled   10 decouple
> *(Suggested answer)*
> 2 Carbon neutral describes products or processes that do not increase the amount of carbon dioxide in the atmosphere, and so have no 'carbon footprint'. (This can be achieved by reducing the consumption of carbon fuels, utilizing alternative energy sources, and by carbon offsetting – balancing or cancelling out the amount of CO_2 emissions through investments in renewable energy, planting trees, etc.)

Economics and ecology **Unit 28**

3 That to reverse global warming it would be necessary to reduce economic activity so much that it would be like going back hundreds of years, or even to prehistoric times (which isn't true, because there are countries where GDP has grown while carbon emissions have declined).

Note

Martin Beniston is an excellent example of the way that native English speakers make great use of the short expressions *you know* and *sort of* as fluency devices in speech. They are, of course, much less frequent in writing.

Listening 3: Can we ignore the problem for now? ▶ 2.27

AUDIO SCRIPT

MARTIN BENISTON I think in some instances the comment can be legitimate, in the sense that one cannot take all actions immediately to counteract climate change, and it's more sort of iterative process, you know, you see climate change kicking in in various regions of the world, then you can start adjusting whatever sector is, needs to be adjusted. On the other hand, you do also have at the same time reasons to act now because of the inertia of the climate system. So the thing is, even if you are rich and you can possibly adjust to that in the future, to some of the negative impacts of climate change in the future, we still need to start acting now to reduce greenhouse gas emissions, because, you know, the more we accumulate GHGs in the atmosphere, the stronger will be warming, and the more negative will be the impact. And many of the impacts are going to affect countries that are still extremely poor, so the sort of countries of the south, basically, which even if they might be richer in tomorrow's world than they are today, will still be poor countries in the next 50 to 100 years, and may not have the economic strength to counteract some of the very negative impacts of climate change like sea level rise or desertification, changes in water resources, and so on.

SUGGESTED ANSWERS

1 Beniston says that Gollier's argument about doing nothing now can be legitimate in some instances, because there are actions that cannot be taken immediately.
2 In many cases it is necessary to act now because of the inertia of the climate system: the more the quantity of greenhouse gases increases, the greater the warming will be.
3 He says that although they might get richer in the next 50 to 100 years, they will still be poor countries that may not be able to counteract the impacts of climate change.
4 The rise of the sea level, desertification, and changes [reductions] in water resources, and so on.

Note

A more usual pronunciation of *iterative* is /ˈɪtərətɪv/.

Discussion

Learners may well have read or seen news items or documentaries about global warming, including *An Inconvenient Truth*, the 2006 documentary directed by David Guggenheim and presented by Al Gore, the former United States Vice President (and winner of the majority of votes in the 2000 presidential election). They will probably know about the threats that global warming presents to their country, and perhaps have some awareness of their country's clean energy policies. This discussion will be all the richer if the learners come from different countries.

Whether and how the learners' countries could increase economic growth while reducing carbon emissions (as Denmark and Sweden have done) is a more technical issue. The final question about reducing economic growth comes back to (and broadens) the Lead-in question in this unit about concern with one's carbon footprint.

Role play: Recommending an energy policy

There are four role cards at the back of the Student's Book on page 154. This role play concerns a developing country because there is probably more leeway as to whether such economies should take the lead in combating global warming.

The learners should be familiar with the overall arguments by now, so all the roles are shown on one page, rather than being spread out on separate pages of the Student's Book. Consequently the learners can also be asked to think of arguments to counter rival proposals they expect to hear in the meeting.

One way to spice up this role play would be to invent an extra role for a contrarian 'scientist' who claims that global warming is not happening, or is not due to carbon dioxide emissions, if you had a learner for whom such a role appeared suitable.

The outcome of the meeting is unpredictable, but the Chairperson should be encouraged to persevere until he/she is able to establish a list of three policy proposals.

Writing

No model answer is given, as the outcome of the meeting is uncertain. The learners could look at the information in the role cards in the Student's Book to help them write their summary.

Thanks and acknowledgements

Although only one name appears on the cover of this book, I need to thank a great many people for their help and hard work, beginning with Cambridge University Press commissioning editor Chris Capper.

Stephanie Ashford, Helen Bicknell, Anna Glinska, Joy Godwin, Graham Jones and Dominique Macabies gave helpful feedback on the previous edition. The outline of this edition was worked out with Chris Capper, Will Capel and Chris Willis.

Will Capel was the development editor, while Chris Willis also made suggestions for the first half of the book and Joy Godwin for the second. Alison Silver also provided ideas throughout, and expertly and good-humouredly prepared the manuscripts for production. Martin Crowdy's expertise was tapped for the units on accounting and finance. All of the editors will find some of their ideas in the book – though I probably scoffed at them at first before managing to convince myself they'd been my ideas all along!

Will Capel set up most of the UK interviews, and Pete Kyle expertly recorded them, with an extraordinarily large microphone on the end of a pole. One other recording was produced by James Richardson. Pete Kyle also produced and edited the CDs. My thanks go to all the interviewees, who graciously gave us their time and shared their expertise with us: John Antonakis, Olga Babakina, Richard Barker, Martin Beniston, Charles Cotton, Carlo de Stefanis, Denis Frucot, Janine George, Melissa Glass, Alan Goodfellow, Anna-Kim Hyun-Seung, Lakshmi Jaya, Michael Kitson, Teresa La Thangue, Alison Maitland, Tony Ramos, Chris Smart, Krishna Srinivasan, Saktiandi Supaat and Rory Taylor. Thanks also go to the writers whose texts I have used, and the cartoonists whose work (mostly from *The New Yorker*) brightens up the pages.

Thanks are also due to Chris Doggett for dealing with permissions, Hilary Luckcock for finding the photographs, Linda Matthews at Cambridge University Press for arranging the production schedule, Wild Apple Design who can and do turn sows' ears into silk purses (as the saying doesn't go), and Kevin Doherty for porof-raeding. Prospective thanks go out to all of Cambridge University Press's sales and marketing people.

I've dedicated previous books to my children, but this time I have to revert to the equally traditional apology-to-partner paragraph: sorry, Kirsten, for the surliness that went with many months of writing a book while also working full-time and taking on too many other commitments. (Oddly, she doesn't believe my assurances that this will never happen again!)

Ian MacKenzie

September 2009

Lightning Source UK Ltd.
Milton Keynes UK
UKHW050942250521
384337UK00001B/2